A Broken Hallelujah

A BROKEN HALLELUJAH

THE MAKING OF A CHRISTIAN BROTHER

LORCAN LEAVY

The
History
Press
Ireland

To the boys and men who shared the Broken Hallelujah with me
in Baldoyle, Marino and Bray.

First published 2012

The History Press Ireland
119 Lower Baggot Street
Dublin 2
Ireland
www.thehistorypress.ie

© Lorcan Leavy, 2012

The right of Lorcan Leavy to be identified as the Author
of this work has been asserted in accordance with the
Copyrights, Designs and Patents Act 1988.

British Library Cataloguing in Publication Data.
A catalogue record for this book is available from the British Library.

ISBN 978 1 84588 739 1

Typesetting and origination by The History Press

CONTENTS

INTRODUCTION

In the formation houses where young Christian Brothers were trained in the 1960s and earlier, an occasion of celebration was called a *Gaudeamus* – from the Latin for 'let us rejoice'. I originally intended to use the term 'A Broken Gaudeamus' as my book title, to reflect both the positive and the negative aspects of that training; a cause for celebration but with some significant cracks in the system. Wiser minds have since convinced me that *A Broken Hallelujah* would be more immediately understandable to potential readers, while at the same time retaining some hint of the conflict between good and not so good which permeated those years of training to become a Christian Brother. The story that follows is an account of events and situations as they happened and existed during the years of my early childhood and merging into the seven eventful years I spent in the Christian Brothers' houses of formation – a time which spanned the 1950s and on into the first half of the 1960s.

I try to describe the world in which I grew up with its own simple richness in order to highlight the contrast between that and the world I inhabited when I left home. My early life could be seen as the seedbed, so to speak, where I and my siblings were nurtured and grew in security and warmth, while the world and the regime I inhabited when I left home could be seen as something of an assault on all that went before. I tell this story to help facilitate understanding of the Christian Brothers and to attempt to cast a critical eye – my own and others' – over what was involved in the making of a Brother.

I also tell it as an account of a personal journey, enriched at one level by a wealth of highly intense experiences and at another level rendered perilous by other, less positive experiences. The recollections of that journey are dependent on the capacity and accuracy of my own memory, their veracity being subject to my own ability to absorb them in the first instance, bearing in mind my youthfulness at the time, and also my ability to recall them, given the passage of many years in the interim. My own possible failure to understand what was happening all around me and the possibility of misinterpretation on my part, would, too, I must admit, colour my telling of these events. However, in so far as I can, I will try to be as accurate as possible.

The story I tell within these pages reflects my own experiences, my feelings, dilemmas, doubts and aspirations. The ideals and values are mine too, as are the regrets, the guilt and the failures. Others may see a different picture when they look back on those days. Their joys and woes may be different to mine, their experiences too. But I can only tell my own story, and I tell it fully conscious and totally respectful of the fact that others may tell it differently.

I hope that truth and understanding are enhanced in some small measure by this exercise.

Lorcan Leavy
January 2012

AT THE
CROSSROADS

So there we were, chugging away in the old Ford
Anglia, destination Dublin; Mam and Dad in the
front, Dad driving, Mam navigating; me and my sister
Anita in the back. As the miles scudded past and the
idyllic countryside faded into the distance while the
threatening bulk of the approaching city loomed, my
heart sank deeper and deeper into my new black shoes.
Was I mad? What had I been thinking? I could have gone
to the local vocational school in Killucan, like everyone
else did; could have studied Woodwork and Rural
Science and Mechanical Drawing as my brothers did,
could have become a mechanic or a carpenter ... but no,
I had to be different. I had to choose an original road – a
secondary school miles from home, a boarding school

at that, and one that set me on a course that would lead to me becoming a member of a Religious Order. The choice had been mine. There was no way out.

Maybe we'll get lost.

Maybe we'll never find the place.

Maybe …

BEGINNINGS

17 January 1946: that was my birthday. I was born at home in Bracklyn in the county of Westmeath, just like all my older brothers and my one older sister. I was the fifth of a family of five – much later to become six. I hated being the youngest, the tag of 'pet' of the family being a difficult one to bear. I feel though, that being the youngest made me fiercely individualistic, always wanting to go my own way, rather than being the scut who tagged along after the rest. I had three brothers: Seán, who was seven years older than me; Mícheál, who was six years older, and Jim, who was five years older. My mother had a few years' rest after Jim. Then came Maureen, and then, eighteen months later, I made my entrance.

Because of the way that our ages ranged, I tended to be 'lumped in' with Maureen, and this I didn't like. I always wanted to be with the boys, doing the things that they were doing. I suppose this made me grow up quickly because in order to keep up with them I was always at full stretch, so to speak, acting beyond my years. I had a summer job at seven years old, for example! Well, to be exact, my brothers had a summer job between them, thinning kale, and for peace sake they allowed me to go with them. But I did learn to do the work, however, and did it right from the beginning. In spite of my best efforts, I never succeeded in being included as one of 'the boys'. This term referred to Seán, Mícheál and Jim. When I was eleven years old, my mother, to her own amazement and to everybody else's, produced a baby girl whom she called Anita. At last, I was no longer the bottom of the pile, the youngest in the house. Anita grew up almost like an only child – everybody's pet and spoiled silly. Unfortunately she was only with us for seventeen years, as she was involved in a traffic accident and died in the summer of 1974.

My father, for his own reasons, wanted to name me 'Mortimor'! My mother vetoed this, saying that it was a silly name. She insisted that I be called Ignatius, even though that was my middle name. My first name was Laurence, after my father, which may have been a consolation for the maternal veto on Mortimor. I hated the name Ignatius so much. I thought that the only people who were named Ignatius were fops and leprechauns. I was nicknamed from the start: Éannaí, which I quite liked; Iggy, which I dreaded (although I don't mind it now). Variations on Iggy were myriad: Iggy the Piggy; Iggywiggy; Iggypops ... One uncle liked to call me Éannaí Biddy Dirt and a cousin called me Ignatius Leprechaun – a fact that I had forgotten until he reminded me of it quite recently. I always swore that at the first opportunity I would change my name, and this I did, but more of that later. I discovered recently, however, that if we went back five generations through my father's family, my great-great-grandfather was called Mortimor. This was shortened to Matt, which has been a family name ever since.

My preschool days were warm and blissful. Precise memories are few; just a feeling of security and warmth. I remember hearing the radio coverage of the Queen's Coronation in England and my mother telling me that she travelled in a golden coach pulled by horses. I also remember hearing, but not necessarily listening to, various programmes on the radio: *Listen with Mother*; *Mrs Dale's Diary*; *Dan Dare and Digby* on Radio Luxembourg.

I remember lots of music too. The name of one group has stuck in my mind from way back then – Edmondo Ros and his band. We didn't have electricity then – I was definitely going to school by the time we got that – so we had light from a blue oil lamp which was hung on the wall of the kitchen. The radio had two big batteries: one operated the radio while the other was being charged in a shop in nearby Delvin.

My mother cooked on an open fireplace, as did most people in our locality at that time. The fireplace had an iron grate with bars across the front and two iron hobs on either side. There was also a crane, from which pots were hung, and it swung out from the fire when necessary. I have a vague memory of bricks or stone surrounding the fireplace, and a high mantelpiece overhead with a serrated valance or pelmet. The iron hobs were always hot and were used for slow cooking or simmering food. Because of all the boiling water and food, and the fire itself, the open fireplace was quite dangerous – a fact of which I became very aware at the age of five, when I pulled a teapot full of scalding tea down on top of myself, resulting in severe scalding on my upper body.

The accident with the teapot gave me a whole new status: I became 'the boy with the scald'. Lots of neighbours called in, with consoling words and cures and holy medals, but more importantly with sweets and biscuits. Unfortunately my mouth was very sore, some splashes of the scalding tea having even got in there, so I couldn't eat much. However, the other children in the house showed remarkable bedside manners and the goodies disappeared a lot faster than it took for my scars to heal over.

I did heal up quite well eventually, except for two troublesome spots on my left arm. 'Proud flesh' started to grow there, which wouldn't allow the areas to heal properly, and so it had to be burned off with caustic acid. This was very painful and frightening, as the flesh sizzled and fizzled like a rasher on a pan – it even smelt like frying meat. Other than the day of the accident, that was the only time I cried – an important fact for a small fellow often referred to as the pet of the family. I have the scars from the scald to this day, including my mother's thumb and index finger prints.

Another strange after-effect of the scald, or rather the healing from the scald, was the fact that the new skin which grew over the damaged areas became very tight, with the result that my arm became permanently bent at the elbow and I was unable to straighten it. So I had to carry something heavy in my left hand for weeks in order to stretch the new skin. The something heavy was usually a hammer. At that time we also had a small hand axe, which I always tried to get hold of (an axe had far more possibilities than a hammer!), but wiser heads decreed that the axe was not allowed.

Shortly after my accident, the fire grate and hobs were taken out and replaced by a beautiful Rayburn range which heated the kitchen and had a fine hotplate and a good big oven for cooking. The Rayburn graced our kitchen for the remainder of our time in Bracklyn – more than fifteen years.

Our house had a kitchen, a back kitchen (utility), two bedrooms and a small pantry, which was pressed into service as a tiny bedroom for Maureen. We also had a parlour, which was used only at Christmas and whenever a visitor called. There were two beds for the four boys in our room; Jim and I shared one, Mícheál and Seán shared the other. We had a small glasshouse at the back which was my mother's pride and joy but it had to be taken down when a new bedroom was built for us boys. Then Maureen moved into our old room. My dad's employer, Captain McCarthy, who owned the house, had a small bathroom built for us – but that's all he did. We had no water supply to the house and he didn't see that we needed it, so we were left with a bathroom with no water, no bath, no toilet, no hand basin … And so it remained, certainly up to the time when I left home in 1959. Until then, our toilet was the wood behind the house and toilet paper was a handful of grass or weeds – whatever was to hand (hopefully not a clump of nettles!).

We had a fine big garden with good black soil where we grew nearly all our food. We all worked in the garden and I suppose we learned a lot there. My three brothers attended the vocational school in Killucan and they all studied Rural Science, during which they had to do a gardening project. They were given a big supply of seeds for a kitchen garden, along with lessons on garden management. At the end of the summer, the Rural Science teacher visited all the gardens and assigned marks to the projects. My brothers won year after year. Personally I believe that their victories were down to me doing so much of the weeding.

We had our own cow, who supplied us with milk and a calf every year. We reared pigs, geese, turkeys and hens, all of which played a role in the economy of our household. The pigs and turkeys and geese were sold for cash, and the hens supplied us with eggs, before eventually ending up in the pot. Preparing the turkeys or geese for the Dublin Christmas market was a big family affair. The birds were despatched to the great turkey roost in the sky by having their necks wrung. It was a bit gruesome but quick and effective. They were then hung up in the cowshed where the plucking took place. We all played a part in this operation and there were many warnings of 'Don't tear the skin!'. The downy feathers were kept for pillows and cushions while the long wing feathers were tied together to make very useful brushes. The rest were burned. My parents prided themselves on how well they 'dressed' the turkeys and they were often complimented on their presentation at the auction.

My mother used to rear chickens from the hatching stage, so our flock of poultry was constantly being renewed. In later years, she bought her replacements as day-old chicks, which arrived in a flat cardboard box with holes in it, on board the Granard bus to Delvin. They were reared indoors, sometimes in our back kitchen, either with a 'clocking' or 'clucking' hen or an infra-red lamp to keep them warm. Occasionally, one of the chicks would get sick and my mother would make a little nest for him in a woollen sock. Having coaxed a few drops of brandy or whiskey into the little patient's beak, she would perch him in his woollen nest under the Rayburn and here, heated within and without, in his drunken slumber he would carry on his own little battle for life, sometimes successful and sometimes not.

We had one cow, as I said; a big, lumbering, gentle Ayrshire. She spent her days in the field behind the house, which we called the Bog Field. Part of my father's terms of employment was that we had the grazing of the Bog Field for our cow. We also played hurling there. At the furthest end of the Bog Field was our spring well, from which we got our drinking water. I never saw that well to go dry, even in the most arid of summers. There were stone steps down to the water and a big smooth rock, about two feet in diameter, in the middle. I often went down to the well on a summer's day after being out playing in the heat. I would lie flat on my tummy on the rock, bring my mouth down to the surface of the crystal-clear water and slurp away to my heart's content. It was never very deep – maybe eighteen inches – so as you lay drinking you could watch the little bugs and beetles scurrying around, some on the surface and some on the bottom. Bringing home water was a constant job that we all had to do. It was quite a long walk from the well, carrying two full buckets. In very hot weather, one of the hazards of bringing home water was the attention of our cow, who would sneak up behind you, stick her big muzzle into the bucket and empty it in one big noisy slurp. Then it was back to the well, with herself waddling along hopefully behind you.

The cow was milked twice a day. I never learned to milk but the boys did. My mother was the best milker

– or at least she got the milk quicker and with less fuss than anybody else. The milk was kept in a basin or crock and when the cream had risen to the top it was skimmed off using a saucer and stored in another crock to be used later for churning butter. Our churn, which consisted of a barrel that revolved on a four-legged stand, held about three gallons of cream and water mix. Everyone had to help with the churning and it certainly made your arms ache. I remember that it used to take forever to make the butter, which I didn't particularly like anyway because it was so salty. There was a little circular glass window on the lid so a practised eye could see when the particles of butter were forming. Then the lid was taken off and the bits of butter were scooped out by hand. We used butter 'hands' to batter the pieces into blocks. I have to admit that I preferred the shop-bought product.

For fresh meat we used poultry (mainly our own chickens), some shop-bought meat and lots of rabbit. These we caught ourselves. This wasn't too difficult, as they were plentiful at the time – indeed too plentiful for the farmers, who regarded them as vermin because they ate their grass and young crops. I always thought rabbit meat was very nice although I heard recently that it is very hard on the digestive system. We seemed to thrive on it anyway.

I suppose, in common with all children, the most magical times in my childhood would have to be the days before, during and after Christmas. Some things we had plenty of – holly, for example. We got our holly from the woods and the house was absolutely bedecked with it. To get a Christmas tree, my dad simply walked back into the wood or out to the edge of the bog and chopped one down. We had some decorations, such as paper chains and the like, which were used year in, year out. They had to be put up with great care and taken down with even more. Fairy lights were unheard of at that time, although my mother used to put a big orange star with an ordinary bulb inside it in the fanlight over the front door. One year, when I was quite small, the local postman, Joe Doyle, who was something of an artist, taught us how to make decorations out of cardboard and tinsel, so a lot of what went on the tree was homemade.

I remember one Christmas in particular – I'd say I was about eight years old – when the kitchen was being redecorated and when I went to bed the place was a shambles; wallpaper torn off the walls, replastering done here and there, no decorations and no tree! I was quite upset because I couldn't see how order would be restored before morning, to say nothing of what Santa would think. However, I eventually fell asleep and it was early morning when I awoke. We scrambled down to the kitchen as we always did on Christmas morning and were greeted by the most beautiful sight we had ever seen – new white wallpaper with a raised floral design in silver, decorations, holly and a fine big Christmas tree. To my childish eyes it was like an ice palace! And Santa Claus was as good as ever. I must have been a bit innocent; I believed in Santa Claus until I was quite big. I got into many a fight defending the good man's reputation. I was a bit hurt when I eventually discovered the truth because I felt they let me take all that flak for nothing. However, I got over it.

There is another Christmas I remember for the lesson it taught me: that childhood doesn't last forever. I was about ten or eleven, I'd say. My brothers were well into their teenage years and had gone out to a dance or to the pictures on Christmas Eve night. Maureen and I were first up on Christmas morning – in fact we were the only ones up, as Mam and Dad never got up early on Christmas morning. The boys were still asleep. Santa had brought us an accordion and I strapped it on and marched up to the boys' bedroom, rattling out my version of 'Fáinne Geal an Lae', only to be met by a stream of swear words which were definitely not in keeping with the Christmas spirit. I was astonished that the boys would rather stay asleep in bed than share the delights of Christmas morning as we always did. I realised then that the magic of childhood was definitely moving on and that it would soon be time for me to move on too.

I think that this sadness stayed with me right through to my last year at home. I was then the only Leavy attending Killough School, since Anita was still only a baby. I used to remember all the fun and adventures we had together; now I was alone.

BRACKLYN ESTATE

My Dad came to Bracklyn at eighteen years of age to work as a herd or stockman. He had to have a helper with him so he brought his younger brother Johnny. For the first few years they lived in Killough, not far from Bracklyn, in the home of their aunt, Mrs Ellen Kelly. Almost forty years later, he was to return to the same house to make it his home after he finished in Bracklyn. Four or five years after starting work in Bracklyn, my father married my mother and they moved into the herd's house, down near Bracklyn Lake.

The old herd's house was completely isolated; there wasn't even a road leading to it. You crossed the fields to get there. My parents lived there for a year, or maybe two, and then they moved to 'our house', where we were all born (except for Anita, who was born in Mullingar Hospital). Even as a child I thought our house was an idyllic place. I often asserted that I would never leave it … although in fact I was the second one to leave and when I left I only returned for one summer holiday over the space of six years. By the time I was eventually free to return, my parents had left the place.

Bracklyn Estate was the ancestral home of the Fetherstonhaughs, an Anglo-Irish family who came to our locality sometime in the late 1600s. The 'lord of the manor' when I was young was Captain James McCarthy, who married into the estate. He came from Herefordshire in England. His wife, Jean Fetherstonhaugh, was a very elegant lady and very friendly – even to us plebeians! The Captain had a fine pedigree herd of Friesian cows and it was in this area that my dad worked. He was in charge of the milk production, the breeding program, and in fact everything that had to do with the cows. One of the many unusual ventures that the Captain initiated was that of milking the cows three times a day. This meant that the first milking took place at about 4 a.m., with a second one at late morning and the third at late evening. My father worked incredible hours but he felt that he didn't have a choice. There were times when we rarely saw him. He would be in bed at about 8 p.m. and up at 3 a.m. He seemed to be always on call for sick animals, calving, or any problems that arose.

Bracklyn House was a relic from the age of the landed gentry and the Big House. It was a huge building with a flight of steps leading up to the front door and down to a terraced lawn. It was built by a Norman family called the Nugents. One of the Fetherstonhaughs 'married in' to a Mary Nugent some time in the 1700s. The only rooms that I remember being in were the hall, the basement and the ballroom. Down in the basement were the old kitchens and the servants' working areas. These were no longer in use when I was a child. I remember their white walls, the very low ceiling and the line of bells, each connected to a particular room upstairs.

The highlight of my limited dealings with the people from the Big House was the annual Christmas Party. The wives and children of all the workers on the estate were invited to a big spread which took place in the ballroom. These occasions made a huge impression on me. We were all scrubbed and decked out in our Sunday best and approached the house with a great deal of awe. To us, these people were all-powerful; we depended on them for our livelihood and even our home. We were welcomed by Mrs McCarthy and the Captain as if we were visiting ambassadors and they lead us into the hall – and there the wonders started. Standing on either side of the door to the ballroom were two giant elephant tusks, mounted onto bases, polished and gleaming. The hall was nearly as big as our house and had a huge staircase leading up to God knows where. I suppose to a child everything seems big, and maybe things weren't really all that big at all, but in the safety of my memory everything in this house was vast. The wooden floor was so polished and shining that we had difficulty walking on it in our good Sunday shoes. Inside the ballroom, tables were laid out with goodies for us and we were served by the staff of the house. I used to be terrified in case I spilled or broke something, but we always really enjoyed the occasion.

After the food, there would have been games or some other activity arranged. One year, they had set up a screen and showed us films. I remember that one film was about golf and another was about germs and the importance of washing your hands. That really went down a treat with us – a gang of forest urchins who considered washing to be a total waste of time and water! The projector kept breaking down, which made the film bounce up and down on the screen – for us this was fun beyond limit and it really brightened up the night's proceedings. Every year, a big net full of balloons was released on us. It seemed like there were millions of them. We all took off our shoes (you couldn't run of the polished floor otherwise) and we whacked those balloons, all million of them, up and down the ballroom. I think we would be there still if our mothers hadn't hauled us off home. As we left, every one of us was given a small present. Magic memories indeed.

Our house in Bracklyn faced across the fields towards the Big House. Four times a day, we heard the bell being rung: for the start of work, for dinnertime, for the resumption of work and for quitting time in the evening. The bell was situated about twenty feet up a beech tree, hanging from a bar which was wedged in place in a fork. At the back of our house were the woods – acres of mature mixed forest. There were beech, ash, oak, sycamore, lime and elm, and some trees the names of which I never knew. There were also lots of coniferous trees, especially Scots Pine. Interspersed through all of this were dense clumps of birch, laurel and rhododendron. The woods were our source of heating fuel, although we did sometimes save turf. We were allowed to cut up and burn any trees that had been blown down in storms or trees that fell from old age. In addition, we could cut wood that might be classified as a nuisance, such as laurel and birch, which grew profusely and spread like weeds. Cutting wood was a constant job in our house, one at which we all took a hand. We used long, two-man crosscut saws to cut up

tree trunks and branches, and then wedges, sledges and hatchets to split the logs into firing. Whenever trees fell across the road to our house or to the Big House, the understanding was that whoever cleared the road got the timber. I can remember weeks of really hard work sawing our way through huge trunks of trees.

One of the most memorable things about Bracklyn House was the walled garden. The surrounding brick wall was twelve or fourteen foot high and inside, there were three separate areas with intervening walls. There was a fruit and vegetable section, a herbaceous area and a rose garden. The gardener was a man called Jim Keegan who lived next door to us. He was an old-style gardener and he knew everything that was worth knowing about flowers and vegetables. It was an idyllic place, full of the scent of fruits and flowers, and wafting through it all was the smell of Jim Keegan's pipe. Jim always had something nice for us whenever we went in – an apple, a plum, some grapes or strawberries. His favourite was a small red apple called Beau of Bath. 'They're small but they're sweet,' he used to say.

SUMMER WORK

One of the fringe benefits of living on Bracklyn Estate was the fact that we were always able to get work during the summer, for which we got paid! There were several options. For a number of years the Captain ran a tulip and daffodil business, selling flowers and bulbs. It was highly labour-intensive work and was probably expensive to run. It lasted for a few seasons and lots of the local young people got several weeks' work as a result.

My favourite job was thinning kale. This was a job that we Leavys got all for ourselves. Kale is a cabbage-like plant used for winter feed for cattle. Some kales have a bushy head of leaves and it is this head which is fed to the animals. Our kale, however, grew a tall, thick, juicy stem with a few skimpy leaves on top. The stem contained the food. The kale seedlings were sown in a continuous line and we had to thin them out, leaving just one plant every nine inches. It was backbreaking work but you could set your own pace and we got quite fast with practice. We were paid 1s 6d (one shilling and six pence) for every hundred yards we thinned. That was approximately 10 cents in today's money. I started thinning kale when I was very young and I worked at it right up to the summer I left home. Because I was a good bit younger than my brothers, I was given the job of lighting a fire every day on which to boil our kettle for making tea. I used to escape the work at twelve o'clock to do this. My brothers were much faster thinners than I was but I used to always aim at doing at least three hundred yards in a day – 4s 6d. The money was all handed up and used to put clothes on our backs for the coming school year. One summer, we also got the job of pulling ragwort (buachalláns) – acres and acres of it. That was a really hard job. The weeds had to be pulled up by the roots, gathered up and stacked on the headlands for collection. The meadows were taller than I was and I used to be wet to my neck if the weather was bad.

SCHOOL DAYS
IN KILLOUGH
NATIONAL SCHOOL

I started school, I think, around 1950 in Killough National School. It was a terrible place; old, decrepit and cold. Both of the teachers were equally old and nearing the end of their careers. My first three years in school were very unhappy. I absolutely hated it. The rod was used on a daily basis, as was common at the time. Misbehaviour and failure at lessons was rewarded with two, four or even six 'of the best' across the open palms of both hands, so it was common to see children nursing their throbbing fingers under their armpits. We were so terrified that I often wonder how anyone learned anything.

The teachers retired within a year of each other and our relief was huge. Our new teacher was a beautiful young lady with whom we all fell in love. Her name was Miss

Fox. She filled the room with pictures and paintings and brightened up the place no end. The other new teacher was Mr Molloy. He was fantastic; unconventional, I think, with hindsight, but always interesting. He was very fond of playing games with us, having competitions, playing hurling and most of all, making music. He played the piano accordion and the saxophone, and he would play for us for hours. He started up a little band in the school, with whistles and accordions and the likes. This was totally novel for the time, even though it's commonplace nowadays. I had my first experience of performing on the stage with that little band. Mr Molloy was a member of The Merry Minstrels Show Band and, as a result of many a late night at the weekends, our Monday mornings were restful in the extreme. On occasion, his colleagues from the band would come to the school and they would have a rehearsal during lunchtime. These tended to be very long lunchtimes, which pleased us greatly.

All the same, I suppose we must have learned a fair bit. He also trained us in hurling and we used to have games against other schools. That was just marvellous. We were fond of our two new teachers and they helped to make school days a good deal less dreadful. I appreciate their work and their influence.

THE BEGINNING OF THE END

By the spring of 1959, I had reached my final year in primary school. The older four of the family were either working or attending second level, while the baby of the family hadn't yet started school. I was preparing to sit my Primary Certificate examination, which was a sort of educational Bar Mitzvah, mercifully no longer in existence, that primary school children had to endure before moving on to the relative adulthood of the secondary school. I had been giving some thought to the direction in which I might go when I finished my time in Killough National School. Would I follow in the footsteps of my three older brothers who had attended the local vocational school and were all serving their time as apprentice mechanical fitters, or would I follow the example of my sister who was in secondary school ... or would some other option present itself? By the month of April, no other option was apparent, but then sometimes in life the most unexpected things can happen.

On the afternoon of Friday 20 April 1959, there came a knock on the school door. The Master opened it and spoke in quiet tones to a stranger whom he ushered into the classroom. He introduced him as a Presentation Brother, who wished to speak to the boys in sixth class. As luck would have it, there were only two sixth class boys in school on that day, the demands of turf-cutting accounting for the rest. I was one of them. As the Brother talked to us about the life and work of the Presentation Order, the seeds of an idea began to sprout in my mind that perhaps this was the other option.

Training to be a Religious Brother would take many years, would involve secular as well as religious education and would demand the successful passage through Intermediate Certificate and Leaving Certificate examinations, as well as teacher training exams, we were told. It was a demanding life but a very worthwhile one, which would guarantee simple happiness now and eternal bliss in the afterlife. There would be the possibility of going to far-flung lands to spread the Word of God. The Brother spoke on, with breathless enthusiasm, about the life he had chosen for himself and into which he hoped to lead one, if not both, of the spellbound boys in front of him. He talked of sacrifice and challenge and the courage required to face both. He quoted from the Bible, 'Leave the dead to bury the dead; your duty is to go and spread the news of the Kingdom of God.' As a final flourish he issued a direct invitation.

'Will you or will you not join the Presentation Brothers in their work?'

My fellow pupil muttered an uncertain, 'I'll have to ask at home,' but I said, 'Yes'.

That was it. The die was cast. Option number three had become the only option.

I was driven home that evening in the Brother's car. He wished to meet my parents, to tell them of the decision already made and to supply them with all the details that would bring the decision to fruition.

How mother Leavy reacted to her youngest son's astonishing announcement that evening is difficult to describe. She had ambitions for her children. She often advised her offspring to keep well clear of farming as a way of life. 'It's all backbreaking work for very little return,' she would tell them. 'Better to get a good nine-to-five job with a weekly wage and some bit of a pension. You know where you are with a weekly wage.'

When her thirteen-year-old son told her that he had decided on his own future and that this would include formal second and third-level education resulting in a profession, she was pleased. The realisation that this profession would be followed in the context of a Religious Order, demanding huge commitment and sacrifice made her a little unsure. She hoped he knew what he was doing, knowing full well that in reality he couldn't, on account of his youth and inexperience. Hopefully God would recognise the generosity of his gesture and protect him.

How father Leavy would react was even less predictable. Larry Leavy was a countryman of the old school, who kept his thoughts and his feelings to himself. He was a man of steel with a heart of butter. While the thought of a lifetime of hard work for the good of humanity appealed to his solidly-held religious convictions, the thought of his young son making such a big decision, and making it so precipitously, filled him with alarm. Like his wife, he would approve of a life based on good education, leading to a generally respected profession. He, too, would approve of a life dedicated to God. But that a boy of thirteen should launch himself on such a path made him feel uneasy.

However, neither he nor his wife was inclined to stand in the way of their son's decision. They would allow him to follow what he so suddenly saw as his calling in life. Who were they to stand in the way of God's great plan for their youngest boy? No, they would go along with it, trust in God and hope for the best.

One thing that did stand in the way, however, was the question of money. Going to the Brothers' Juniorate in Cork would involve the payment of fees and the amount was beyond what my parents saw as being within their capabilities. My father stood firmly by his conviction that they could not possibly raise the sum discussed and for a moment or two there appeared to be an impasse. Much to their surprise, however, the visitor suggested that if the payment of fees was not possible then they should look at an Order of teaching Brothers whose fees, where they existed, would be set at whatever level the family could pay. The Order in question, he said, was the Irish Christian Brothers, and he gave my parents a contact address.

Some days later, Mam, Dad and I sat round the kitchen table to compose a letter to the Irish Christian Brothers. This was a laborious task; they weren't quite sure whether they were announcing their wish for their son to join the Order or if they were asking the Order to accept their son. However, the letter was written and it had the desired effect. In due course, the family was graced with another visit, this time from an Irish Christian Brother, who outlined arrangements and plans.

A few weeks later a letter from the Christian Brothers arrived with details of everything I would need when I went to the Brothers' Juniorate, and it initiated a shopping spree the likes of which I had never seen before. A black suit, a black pullover and pants, black shoes and socks, a black overcoat, on and on the list went; a toothbrush, toothpaste, several sets of underwear, white shirts, black ties, football boots, swimming trunks and so on. In the Leavy house everything was shared or else handed down, but now I was to be kitted out with my very own set of possessions. As the time passed and my store of belongings increased, so the element of choice seemed to disappear and a sense of foreboding began to grow. My parents had gone to such expense to kit me out. There was no way I could back out now.

During the few minutes in which I made my decision in Killough National School, I was in charge. Now my decision appeared to be in charge of me and I began to feel trapped. And in this unsure frame of mind, I continued to prepare for the big departure. As if sensing the enormity of the change ahead of me, I luxuriated in the summer days of 1959, the rustic setting that was home, the normal activities of a young, country lad. But 18 August moved inexorably closer and eventually it arrived.

18 AUGUST, THE LEAVING AND THE ENTERING

In later years, my memories of the moment of leaving my rural home in the Irish midlands were scarce to the extent of being non-existent. I retained no memory of saying goodbye to my brothers. I had always looked up to them. They led the way and I trotted along behind but now I was set on a course all of my own choosing, with nobody walking ahead to warn me of dangers and to help me over difficulties. So intense was my internal turmoil that I was unable to imagine how they would be feeling as they watched their youngest brother head off on his great adventure.

But the leave-taking happened and the large suitcase containing all my newly bought possessions was strapped to the roof of the Ford Anglia, and away we went, Dad driving, Mam navigating and sister Anita sharing the back seat with a tremulous me.

A trip to Dublin from the midlands in the late 1950s was in itself quite an undertaking and not one to be embarked upon lightly. Those in rural Ireland who were lucky enough to own a car had to be satisfied with a very second-hand second-hand model, so successfully reaching any destination without mechanical problems of some kind could never be presumed. The drive from Westmeath to Dublin and back was a noteworthy undertaking. And for a driver who was accustomed only to the quiet, if winding, roads of the midlands, to face the terrors of city traffic and all that goes with it, well, that was the stuff of nightmares.

Dad coped well with the roads of County Meath and the small towns he had to pass through as he made his way towards the city – Ballivor, Rathmolyon, Summerhill, Dunboyne – but as the first city bus trundled in his direction, he was no longer in his natural element. He soon found himself driving in double and even treble lanes of traffic, and over the course of several hours he traversed Dublin city, cursing his dodgy handbrake and hoping that his battery wouldn't go flat or that his engine wouldn't stall with all the stop-go movement of the city traffic.

As the tension rose in the front seats, silence descended on the back. My courage had more or less deserted me and as the search for the Brothers' college in Baldoyle continued fruitlessly, I allowed myself to hope that, maybe with a little bit of luck, they would never find the wretched place and that we would return to the quiet and sleepy midlands, glad to have survived this flirtation with lunacy.

But find it they did; a tall house on a narrow street, looking out towards the Irish Sea, with some stone steps leading up to an elegant front door. Realising that the time for doubts was now past, I stood in my black suit and shiny shoes alongside my parents and sister as Dad rang the doorbell. All too soon, for me, came the sound of approaching footsteps. The door was opened by a tall man dressed in a long, black soutane. Introductions followed and our small group was ushered into a large and immaculately tidy parlour. The words that were exchanged over the course of the following fifteen or twenty minutes failed to register in my consciousness. I struggled to deal with the ambience of this new place, so totally different from our own little house, on the edge of a forest, facing out onto acres of midlands farmland. This room had a high ceiling, spartan but expensive-looking furniture, with no vestige of softness or decoration, and an invasive smell of wax polish. All the surfaces were gleaming, as if every trace of femininity or even humanity had been buffed out of them. My father seemed to have taken a liking to the gaunt Br Paul, and the two engaged in relaxed and easy conversation.

We were then taken on a brief tour of the college, which Br Paul referred to as 'the house'. That a building so vast and rambling could be referred to as 'the house' amazed me. A winding corridor brought us to the refectory, an extraordinary place in my view, with lines of long tables all set for the next meal and a table on a raised rostrum where the Brothers on the staff had their meals. With some astonishment, I was later to learn that the boys were not allowed to look at the 'Top Table' during the course of their meals!

Then we were shown into the chapel. Another extraordinary thought; a private chapel inside a house. It had rows of wooden pews on both sides of a stone-tiled central aisle, lit moodily by stained-glass windows and dominated by the altar at one end and a pipe organ high up in the gallery at the other. It would be easy to be saintly in a place like this.

Next, we visited the dormitories. These were several long corridors with a row of cubicles on either side, each one accessed by means of a passage down the centre.

Every boy was assigned his own cubicle, which could be closed for privacy by means of a curtain across the front. In each one there was a bed, a small wardrobe and an old-fashioned washstand containing a basin full of cold water, a soap tray and a chamber pot. Always having had to share with my brothers, the idea of my own private cubicle seemed luxurious. The corridors were named after various saints – St Kevin's corridor, St Fintan's corridor, and so on.

The study was a long, large room with about eighty desks arranged in neat rows. At one end was a huge fireplace, which looked as if it never was used. Some table-tennis tables occupied the space behind the desks and several tall book presses stood against the back wall. At the head of the room there was a large desk mounted on a high platform. Each boy would have his own desk at which to read and study, we were told, as well as a cubbyhole located on the wall in which to store his books. The book presses contained part of the well-stocked house library. When I was introduced to some boys in the study they greeted me with the words, 'Welcome to Baldoyle' – a salutation that on one hand made me feel welcomed, but on the other, a bit imprisoned.

And then it was back down to the parlour by a different flight of stairs, where my parents and sister took their leave to face the tortuous trek through the city and back to their little house on the edge of the forest. The moment of parting was so traumatic for both my family and me, that memory of it was promptly obliterated from my mind, never again to be revisited. How my parents must have felt, I had no idea – in fact, so preoccupied was I with the newness and the strangeness of my surroundings, and the challenges facing me, that I was incapable of giving any thought at all to my family's feelings.

This place was so big! How would I ever find my way around it? This big house was to be my world for the future; the place where I would sleep, eat, wash, dress, work, play and pray. I would share this space with my new family because my old family was now very, very far away. The truth of this latter fact would become clearer to me as time went on but even as of now, on my first day, I could get some sense of it, of the way that the structure of the place and the regime followed in it would create a vast chasm between me and my home and family. They may have been only fifty miles away but in practical terms I may as well have taken up residence on the dark side of the moon. Already I knew that there would be no holidays at home until the following summer, a full year away. I also knew that visits from my family would be strictly limited and that my monthly letters home would be handed up unsealed and their contents read before despatch. All incoming letters, though unlimited in number, would also be opened and read by the Superior before being passed on to each boy. But I wasn't to know yet that in the common parlance of the Brothers' Order anyone who wasn't a Christian Brother was referred to as 'an extern', with a subtle implication that contact of any kind with externs was to be avoided where possible. Where the externs were not members of the boys' immediate families, then contact was simply not allowed.

So settling into my new family and my new home became the purpose of the moment for me. And since that was what needed to be done, for the immediate future anyway, it was well that I set about my purpose with energy and commitment. And that I did.

LIFE IN THE JUNIORATE

Over the course of the next few days, routines became familiar, as did the geography of the building. Schoolwork wouldn't start for another week, so each new boy had ample time to settle in and to get to know his new companions. St Joseph's, Baldoyle, was the Juniorate for the Brothers' Order catering for the northern half of the country, that is, north of a line from Dublin to Galway. Boys who came from south of that line had their Juniorate in Dún Laoghaire. Those attending Juniorate were known as postulants, from the Latin '*postulare*', meaning 'to demand'. So they were demanding entry to the Order of the Christian Brothers, and the Juniorate both prepared them for this and assessed their suitability.

I was assigned my cubicle in St Kevin's corridor and was given time to unpack my suitcase and to arrange my new world to my own satisfaction. The empty case was stowed away against the wall at the head of the bed and already, even then, as I looked at it I longed for the day when I would pack it again and head off home. However, thoughts of this nature were not to be indulged. I was here now and here I would stay, and come hell or high water, I would survive.

The free week before the start of formal classes was very pleasant, with lots of leisure time, walks, games, swimming in the sea and even a trip to Chipperfield's Circus; enough time for the new boys to become accustomed to their new status as Religious in training. But while the days were busy and interesting, it was at night-time that the doubts and loneliness came back. They robbed me of my sleep and left me fighting back the tears, which were never very far away in those days. At first I wondered if I would ever sleep, with the constant hum of the city traffic and the street lights that shone through the window of the cubicle, even in the dead of night. At home, the nights were dark and quiet, apart from the occasional yelping of a passing fox as he tested the night for the presence of dogs. But as time passed by, I became accustomed to the noise and the night-time lights.

The sense of being in the world but cut away from the world – like a drop of oil in a vessel of water – I found difficult to cope with. Outside of this microcosm, normal life went on. From the top-storey window of St Joseph's, one could see people coming and going at the Little Willie Hospital, clutching their bags of grapes and their bottles of Lucozade. Beyond that could be seen Baldoyle Racetrack, where people ate their choc ices and placed their bets, cheered on their winners and cursed their losers. Men clipped their hedges and tended their borders as the long phalanx of black-clad boys, with their rolled-up towels tucked under their arms, walked past on their way to the beach at Sutton, barely daring to look for fear of reawakening some illicit longing already well on its way to being stifled.

One week after arriving in Baldoyle, the onset of official classes signalled the start of a strictly timetabled routine. This proved to be, at one and the same time, a godsend, in that it filled every minute of the waking day, but also an inflexible oppression, in that it left no free time for daydreaming. In fact, daydreaming time was considered to be at best undesirable and at worst, downright dangerous.

The day started early and finished early. The wake-up bell was rung with great energy along each of the corridors at seven thirty, followed by morning prayers and Mass in the chapel, celebrated by a Capuchin priest with a deep, sonorous voice. Each boy returned to his cubicle after Mass to make his bed and generally tidy up. This was followed by breakfast, which was eaten in silence while one of the boys read aloud from a spiritual book. Then on to a half hour of frantic housekeeping – with each boy assigned a particular chore or 'charge', as well as the scrupulous cleaning and tidying of his own cubicle.

Formal classes started at nine o'clock and broke for the main meal, part of which was eaten in silence. Classes resumed in the early afternoon for a further two hours, finally finishing at four o'clock. This was followed by football – in all sorts of weather – for an hour. A light snack followed in the refectory and then it was down to study for two hours. Then the final meal of the day was eaten, followed by three quarters of an hour of 'recreation' – the only time during the course of the day when the boys had free time to call their own. But even then, recreation time had to be spent in a specific place and had to comprise specific activities. At the end of this time, we went to the chapel for night prayers prior to bedtime. Lights were switched off at ten o'clock.

There was no 'leeway' time in between the various elements of the timetable, with the end of one activity and the beginning of another signalled by a single ringing of the bell. Moving from one activity to another, when it did involve movement – and it nearly always did – was therefore best undertaken at something of a gallop. Punctuality was highly regarded and lateness was not tolerated, hence the urgency. Formal classes were held on six out of the seven days, with two extended periods of study on Sundays.

A long walk around the coastal area of Baldoyle and Sutton was also a fixed arrangement on Sunday afternoons. The boys walked in groups of three in a long procession, with a specific distance between each trio and at a specific speed so that no group could pass the group ahead. Even the make-up of each group of three was decided by the Brother in charge, as was the route. The postulants were strictly forbidden from 'speaking to externs' while out walking. In fact, their time outside the walls of the house was governed by a monastic rule called 'custody of the eyes', by which Religious were required to avert their eyes from anything which might be detrimental to their spiritual welfare. With our completely black attire and our downcast eyes, we must have looked very strange to the local population.

THE DOOR
CLOSES

Once the hand is laid on the plough, no one who looks back is fit for the Kingdom of God.

Luke 9:62

Very early in my time in my new home, I was to come to realise the seriousness of the decision I had made so hurriedly in Killough National School some months earlier. At the end of classes every day, the Superior, Br Paul, addressed the boys from his elevated desk – known, for some reason, as the 'Dickie' – at the head of the study. This daily talk concerned matters of practical housekeeping, announcements, directions and corrections ('It has come to my notice that some boys are …'), and also an element of spiritual teaching on the life that would be expected from us fledgling Religious during our current term as trainees, and later during our lives as Christian Brothers. One of the first lectures I listened to was on the topic of vocation – the notion that the reason I was in this house, following this way of life, was that God had called me to be here and that I had answered his call. This divine invitation was known as a vocation, we were told. We were also told that since we had answered God's call, we were no longer free to even consider leaving, since to do so would be tantamount to throwing God's invitation in his face. I had never even heard the word 'vocation' before and the whole idea filled me with delight, on the one hand, that I had been so fortunate as to be chosen, but also with terror at the thought that I was no longer free to change my mind. This message of following one's religious vocation was one I would hear repeated with great emphasis many more times in the days, months and years ahead. In fact, so central was the notion of 'following one's vocation' and not 'losing one's vocation', that to me it appeared to resemble a metal scaffold supporting and giving meaning to the life we were living, but also a metal cage holding us captive and isolating us from huge swathes of normal life.

The enormity of the commitment involved was epitomised in the telling of an often-repeated, apocryphal story. It concerned an overheard conversation between two overawed country boys as they surveyed their situation in Baldoyle. One was heard to enquire of the other, 'Are 'ou glad 'ou come? Do 'ou think 'ou'll shtick?'

To me, however, at this early stage in my experience, the difficulties and sacrifices apparent in my chosen way of life were far from insurmountable. I glowed with youthful energy in the face of it all and luxuriated in the religious commitment demanded from me. I threw myself into both work and play with equal enthusiasm and soon learned to relax in my new environment.

I was to discover, too, that the level of teaching in Baldoyle was of a very high, if somewhat strange, standard indeed. Instruction was imparted with the absolute minimum of confusion. Here was instruction that was completely subject centred, stark, clear and, where possible, simple. Only what was likely to appear on an exam paper was dwelt on and rote learning formed the basis of much that was imparted to us. There wasn't much sign, in this educational establishment, of liberal or lateral learning. Instead, the facts were presented in as simple a manner as possible and where appropriate were committed to memory with the aid of whatever mnemonics and learning aids as could be devised by clever and skilled teachers.

This sparse and trimmed-down curriculum was driven home in some situations by the liberal use of corporal punishment; no leather straps or canes in this school, rather the bare hand or even the closed fist. One Brother in particular seemed to believe that every boy needed a good thump from time to time, and if a justifiable excuse for it did not present itself then he would invent one. The same Brother was a gifted teacher who dispelled confusion and presented his material in a thoroughly organised and well-prepared manner. However, his almost manic drive and temper outbursts inspired terror in all who sat in front of him. The fact that everybody learned very well from him was a testament to his teaching skills but also to the aggression and violence which permeated his practice as a teacher.

For the most part, the other Brothers on the teaching staff were gentle and kind in their dealings with us, if you discount the man who would rap one violently with his knuckles on the top of the head for any breach of the rules. Then there was the one who specialised in pinching the cheek of any unfortunate who failed at his lessons or who misbehaved in any way. He would bury his thumbnail into the nipped flesh and so many of us carried black and blue bruises on our faces as a token of our dealings with 'the Pincher'. However, it seemed both of these men tried to administer their reprimands in an almost jocular way, making them appear more like horseplay than real punishment.

For all that I feared corporal punishment, I found the minimal and uncluttered approach to teaching to be much to my liking. The clarity with which the material was presented did much to clear away years of confusion left over from my days in primary school. Here things made sense. There was logic and consistency to the subjects taught. I learned well and quite enjoyed the experience.

The ever-present threat, though, of the fist-pummelling punishment did cause me some disquiet and occasionally robbed me of my night's sleep. This was not like the cane on the outstretched hand delivered reluctantly by my old primary school teacher, who seemed to suffer more in the delivery than the pupils did in the receiving. This was personal and left the unfortunate recipient humiliated and violated. For me, this threat and the fear it gave rise to cast a long shadow over my years in Baldoyle. But while I feared the tempestuous Brother, I held him in such high regard that I would willingly have crawled on my hands and knees for the slightest sign of approval and appreciation from him.

In the Juniorate, there were about seventy boys who came from practically every county in Ireland, north of a line from Galway to Dublin. For me, it was a great experience, living at close quarters with lads from such diverse backgrounds. There were boys there from cities – Dublin, Galway, Belfast and Derry – and from towns like Newry, Tullamore, Mullingar, Sligo, Westport and so on. There were also a small number from country places, as I was. Some, myself included, joined very young, with little or no knowledge of the world, while others joined at an older age – fourteen or fifteen. Many of these would be quite worldly wise, especially if they were city boys. Some tended to be slightly ghetto-minded and only mixed with people from their own home towns, but I got on well with most people and tried to be a good mixer.

The subject choice for the Intermediate Certificate was very simple: everyone did Irish, English, Mathematics (pass level), Geography, History, Latin and Mechanical Drawing, with a small number studying Science. The range on offer seemed to have more to do with the aptitudes of the teachers than the needs or wishes of the students.

Every boy in Baldoyle became a member of the choir, learning and performing a range of choral music, mostly of a religious nature. The choirmaster was the redoubtable 'punching' Brother, who beat the finer points of Latin and Irish grammar into us in another context. Here, again, his teaching methods were hugely effective and his standards impossibly high. The slightest error would draw down an ear-splitting slap on the face or a drum roll of punches. While enduring the fear resultant from his methods, we did learn much about Plain and Gregorian Chant and two and four-part harmony singing.

The same Brother set up an orchestra, which consisted of whatever musical abilities were available to him in any particular year. The mainstay of the orchestra was the first and second violins along with, incredibly, two groups of tin whistles, added to by drums and percussion, two cellos, piano and organ, and any other instrument available, like trumpet, clarinet and piano accordion. Musical arrangements were prepared by the Brother to match the playing and reading ability of each student and the overall outcome was impressive. During the course of the two years that I spent in Baldoyle, the orchestra performed themes from *The Mikado*, the 'Barcarolle' from *The Tales of Hoffman*, *Funiculi Funiculà*, Tchaikovsky's piano concerto and others, along with some popular tunes like 'The Wandering Minstrel'. In my first year I played the drums and percussion, and in the second year I was promoted to the cello. Because I hadn't yet learned to read music, the Musical Director devised an ingenious system of notation, which made it possible for me to play both.

I struggled to understand why a man of such brilliance would feel the need to terrify and bully those he taught. I remembered my former teacher in Killough who would punish reluctantly and with obvious distaste. He would occasionally lose his temper but would clearly feel bad about it afterwards. But this man exploded on a daily basis – almost as if a loss of self-control and the violence this lead to was regarded as a chosen element of his own personal style of teaching.

I had succeeded in keeping my head down and avoiding the worst of his fury to the extent that I began to think that maybe, for some reason, I was not going to be targeted. However, the dark cloud that hung over the place was destined to burst when I least expected it. It was the custom for the boys, whenever they had finished their charges in the morning, to hurry to the study to prepare for the day's classes. This particular morning, the Brother stomped into the hall, produced a piece of paper and called out five names, including mine, and instructed us to follow him. Down in St Kevin's corridor, our first stop was at my cubicle. We were shown the light layer of dust on top of the wainscoting and the tiny rolls of fluff that I had failed to remove from under the bed. The outcome was inevitable. Slaps and punches rained upon me as I was pushed into a corner. I had never experienced anything like this before. Yes, I had had the occasional slap at home or in school but not like this – a sustained physical assault from an adult, and an adult, at that, wearing a clerical collar. The strident verbal tirade which accompanied it added to the intensity, so that I felt fear, outrage and humiliation all at once.

Afterwards, I tried to rationalise the incident. I asked myself questions that I could never expect to have answered. Why was he so angry? What did I do, or fail to do, to warrant such an extreme reaction? Who gave him the right to terrify me? He is supposed to be following the God of love, yet he beat me with his fists on account of a few wisps of dust. And I am powerless. I have to meet him again in the Latin class and again in the Irish class, and I am not allowed to respond in any way. He has all the power. Is this fair? I even entertained the futile thought that this wouldn't be allowed to happen if my dad was here. And the most astonishing thing of all was that it *was* allowed to happen, on almost a daily basis. Today it was me, tomorrow it would be someone else. Nobody told him to stop, or if they did, he ignored them. Neither his colleagues on the staff nor his Superior appeared to be aware or to care. So was this regarded as acceptable behaviour? Was this the norm? It was well known among the boys that, while it appeared to be alright to beat the boys in Baldoyle, once they moved on to the Novitiate and donned the habit of the Christian Brothers, there would be no more physical punishment. Did this mean that there was belief that only those in religious garb were worthy of respect? Or was this evidence of a belief that a bit of a 'roughing up' was actually good for a boy, an essential part of his education? These were questions which would remain unanswered, no matter how I addressed them in the days, months and years that followed.

I was to spend two years in Baldoyle and while the regime was very severe and personal freedoms were much curtailed, I was very happy there most of the time. I decided that since the decision to come here was my own, I had better make the best of it. I decided to accept the regime as it was presented to me, that this was the path down which I had to travel in order to achieve my aims. I realised very early in my experience that as long as I conformed to the system as it was put before me, I would have no problems. But the system was designed to isolate me from home and family, from the outside world, from what could be seen as normal secular life, because normal secular life was regarded as being inferior to Religious Life and every element of normal secular life – sexuality, marriage and parenthood especially – was seen as greatly inferior to the corresponding elements of Religious Life.

I wouldn't fight against it, I told myself. I would simply go along with it. And consequently I had very little hassle or strife. All in all, life was good.

At this early stage, being still only thirteen years old, I was unaware and unconcerned about any negative effects that a life of such denial and withdrawal would, or could, have on my emotional and psychological wellbeing. I had no reason to doubt the wisdom or the intentions of the Brothers – it was, after all, a time in Irish life when one neither doubted nor suspected Religious or priests. It had already been instilled in me that the voice of my Superior was the voice of God and that this demanded blind and unquestioning obedience. As yet, on account of my youthfulness, I had not become aware of the usual turmoil the onset of puberty could bring. Later, I would conclude that this was the reason why the Brothers liked to enrol very young boys; the belief that it would be easier to mould the minds and lives of young and impressionable people – blank canvases, so to speak – than to undo and obliterate the influences of what was seen as the inferior and sinful society outside the realm of their Order.

Not everything in Baldoyle was negative – far from it. There were many manifestations of genuine care and concern for the boys' welfare, in spite of the ever-present threat of physical punishment. Br Paul showed himself to be a kind and caring Superior, who made a fleeting visit to every boy in his cubicle after night prayers to make sure they were alright. He also had a face-to-face meeting with each boy every month in his office, at which problems and questions were dealt with in an avuncular manner. Apart from a small initial payment, my parents were never asked to contribute financially to my up-keep or education. In fact, as clothes and such like began to wear out, they were replaced free of charge by the Brothers.

Other things enriched our lives in the Juniorate, like the opportunity to study violin or piano, to perform on the stage in music and drama, and to be part of the orchestra. But all of this was part of a policy of training, training to perform in a particular role – that of a teaching Christian Brother. It was training rather than education; training the boys to do certain things because in the future that the Order had mapped out for them, these things would need to be done. The focus appeared to be on the role rather than the person who would fill the role. The training would effectively wipe out the person and all his human and undesirable inclinations, while equipping him with the skills deemed necessary to make him an efficient Christian Brother. And the efficient Christian Brother would be trained to be a good and dedicated teacher, a constructive and useful member of his religious community, would say his prayers, live according to the precepts of his religious Rule and obey his Superiors. That he might be socially, emotionally or sexually stunted was a consequence hardly addressed, nor was the danger, the likelihood even, that his individuality, his unique personality, might be more or less negated in the process. The skills and aptitudes deemed to be desirable in a Christian Brother would also include proficiency in the Irish language, a fervent and inward-looking dedication to the ideals of Irish nationalism, and involvement with and support for the Gaelic Athletic Association. It would also require a degree of no-nonsense and unemotional toughness in our dealings with each other and with outsiders. The drop-out rate over the years of training would be more than 90 per cent, however, and therefore very few of the boys being so aggressively trained would actually live the life for which they were being prepared. How those who left would cope with life as laymen in the outside world, after being cloistered so exclusively during their most formative years, was anybody's guess. The Order appeared to believe that this matter need not concern them; if boys left, they left, and on their heads be it.

All eventualities of daily life were catered for in Baldoyle. The laundry was spirited away every week and reappeared, spotless and folded, some days later. I would wonder, in later years, if this work was dealt with in a Magdalene Laundry, but this I never investigated, preferring not to know if my washing added to the burden of the poor women who worked in those institutions. A small room equipped with a sewing machine was set aside for the periodic visit of a seamstress who performed restorative miracles on the knees and elbows of the boys' clothes. Br Paul was constantly urging us to get our clothes mended, 'and not to be going round lookin' like ragamuffins'.

A whispered plan took root – it was never clear from where it evolved – to take Br Paul at his word and to inundate the unfortunate seamstress with every possible repair job imaginable. As the appointed day approached, a steady stream of boys could be seen, bundles of clothes in hand, making their way to the seamstress's room. Normally, the work requiring attention was left on a worktop inside the door, but on this occasion not only was the worktop full, but the room was full, and the bundles of clothes with their noted requests attached spilled out the door onto the corridor outside. A great degree of ingenuity was used in the composition of the notes. A note with a button attached read, 'Please sew a trousers on to this button.' Another requested, 'Please connect these two tears with a shirt.' Another note, with nothing attached, read, 'Please repair this hole.' Poor Br Paul had to draw on all his conciliatory skills to prevent a walkout by the seamstress. Thankfully, she didn't leave, much to the relief of boys and Brothers, because apart from being incredibly skilled at her trade, she was most obliging and helpful. All in all, we were a bit ashamed that our little joke had assumed such gargantuan proportions. The Superior was incandescent with rage over it, but like everything else, it soon blew over.

Another monthly visitor was the barber. He appeared to believe that it was his God-given mission to rid these would-be Brothers of all vestiges of human pride, because he chopped and hacked our hair to such an extent that we looked as if we had just emerged from under a moving lawnmower. This operation usually took place during evening study, and as each red-faced victim re-entered the study, with his few wisps of remaining hair sticking torturously out of his tonsured skull, the magnum opus was greeted with howls of laughter – laughter somewhat muted by the knowledge that the same fate, or worse, awaited everyone. Even some of the Brothers subjected themselves to the manic ministrations of the barber. When Br Paul attempted to remonstrate with him that he might 'go a little easier on the lads', the response was, 'Do they want to be Christian Brothers or "musicianers"?'

During my first year in Baldoyle, the practice of personal hygiene was somewhat primitive, if efficient. Since there were no facilities for showers or baths, washing consisted of an early morning scrub over a basin of cold water, with a weekly 'big scrub', which was carried out as follows: in each dormitory one boy was given a tub of scalding hot water and a large jug; all the other boys would line up with their empty basins to be topped up with hot water by the wielder of the jug; they would then carry their offering back to their cubicle, where they would use it to wash 'as far up and as far down' as their reach and general flexibility made possible. This surprisingly simple and effective practice was discontinued in year two, when a whole bank of new showers was made available.

As the year moved into late autumn, the boys were occasionally allowed to leave their classroom for a day and to go out to work on the Brothers' farm. This really delighted the lads from the country, reminding them of home and allowing them to feel in their element, so to speak, even though they were in an otherwise urban, and therefore alien, setting. Potatoes needed to be picked and turnips snagged because the produce of the farm was needed to sustain all who lived in the Juniorate.

From time to time, the monotony of life for the postulants was eased by the announcement that we would be having a film show. The school owned a 16mm film projector, and with the help of one of the many companies who rented out 16mm films, the boys would have an evening to remember. Various black-and-white films were shown but the accepted favourites on all occasions were a number of cartoon and comedy shorts, which the school owned. Among these was one called *Spills & Thrills*, which portrayed the ultimate in comedy – the falls, crashes and disasters of the silent screen.

The steady throb of life in the Juniorate went on more or less smoothly and soon Christmas was approaching. The boys from Dublin were allowed home for a day or two during the holiday but the country boys had to stay. This was my first Christmas away from home and it was the first Christmas for my family with an empty chair at the table. I still hadn't reached my fourteenth birthday and I found it heart wrenching to think that I wouldn't share the Christmas cheer with my parents and siblings. As my peers and I walked along the Coast Road, we could see people setting up their decorations and Christmas trees in their sitting rooms; but we would have to return to the cavernous halls and long corridors of the medieval building which had now taken the place of our homes.

Without access to radio, television or newspapers (with the exception of the local newspapers, which families were allowed to send to the boys) the postulants' principal experience of Christmas would be a religious one. And while I found the religious aspect of Christmas as presented in Baldoyle to be very meaningful and very moving, I missed my family and the festivities I had enjoyed at home. However, cards and presents were received and the Brothers, themselves victims of a rigid system, did their utmost to give us all as good a time as was possible within the limitations of the formation structure as enforced by their own Superiors. We had the best of Christmas food, and for boys by now unused to culinary luxuries, the Christmas plate was luxurious indeed. Good food, games, free time, some decorations and a Christmas tree all combined to help us forget – at least during the daylight hours – that our families were light years away. But even in the aftermath of Christmas, as we made our way along the Coast Road, the sight of discarded Christmas decorations protruding from the dustbins caused a lump in many a throat.

The New Year ushered in the brave new world of the 1960s, but for the boys in St Joseph's nothing would change. The routine was still supreme, with prayers followed by work followed by study followed by football followed by prayers. As the fresh winds of economic revival lifted the outside world out of the sad embrace of recession, we still were immersed in our God-centred, heaven-directed milieu, as we were taught to despise the world, the flesh and the devil present around us and inside us.

We were strictly forbidden from having 'particular friends', that is, exclusive friendships confined to just one other person. This would appear to suggest that there was some awareness among the designers of the program of formation being imposed on us that there were dangers associated with a celibate life. They appeared to fear that if the sexual impulses that are part of normal human nature are suppressed or denied, then they will seek expression in other ways. This denial of the right, or indeed the need, to have close and exclusive friendships caused heartache for some of the boys, including myself, who experienced loneliness in the midst of a group most of whom I regarded as friends. And when I did form close personal friendships, I was wracked with guilt and fear of punishment from those in charge. Bearing in mind that we were still only in our early teens, and that we would be subject to the rigorous implementation of this prohibition on close friendships for at least the next six years, an observer would be forgiven for wondering if we would not eventually lose the capacity for close friendship. Given that the aim of the training in the Juniorate, the Novitiate and afterwards was to instil in us an almost automatic preference for certain ways of behaving and an equally automatic revulsion for other ways, it would hardly be surprising if our need for friendships and our ability to form relationships would inevitably suffer. This rule was known by its Latin name, *noli me tangere*, meaning 'do not touch me', which were the words addressed to Mary Magdalene by the risen Christ. In an ironic case of sideways application, the Christian Brothers applied it to their rule banning close, exclusive friendships.

Another absolute in the day-to-day rules governing the lives of the boys in Baldoyle was the prohibition on any boy from entering another boy's cubicle, with or without his permission. In lots of ways, this rule was welcomed by all of us, as it guaranteed our one small corner of privacy. But the great absolute of all was that of the night silence. From the end of night prayers to the start of morning prayers, the boys were forbidden to speak or to communicate with each other in any way – the only exception being when the Superior briefly visited each cubicle. Indeed, much of the day was spent in silence but the night silence was enforced most rigorously. The hope was that night-time would be shared only with God, but in my case God had to be willing to share the time with my parents and family. No matter how busy the day was and no matter how tired I was, the memory of my family and my home came flooding back after the bell for lights out ushered in the night. As time went on, though, the past played a less and less significant role in my consciousness and the present, with its new surroundings and new companions, became a more central element in my life. Even the few family visits which were allowed during the year, although greatly anticipated and appreciated, did little to distract from the total absorption in this new life that I was experiencing. And as the summer of 1960 and my first holiday at home in a year approached, I wondered if I would feel out of place in my old house and if I would miss the structure and security of life in the Juniorate.

A HOLIDAY
AT HOME

The summer holidays arrived and my friends and I were dispatched homewards on the train with great glee and anticipation. And I did, to an extent, feel out of place in the middle of the cut and thrust of family life. It was only in the context of home and family that I became aware of just how much I had changed. So well indoctrinated was I that I felt the need to continue to wear my black clothes while at home, to attend daily Mass and to say the usual prayers I had become accustomed to saying in Baldoyle. Unsurprisingly, then, I felt like an outsider here; one who visited but didn't really belong. And it surprised me even more that as the time to return to Baldoyle approached, I didn't regard it with dread, as I had thought I would, but rather with anticipation. The fact that I wouldn't be allowed to visit home again for at least five years didn't really dull this keenness. I would be one of the 'old boys' now and it would be my role and privilege to welcome the new boys and help them to settle in.

But some boys didn't return to the Juniorate. This shocked me. That anyone would even consider giving up on his vocation was a matter of some amazement to me; for anyone to act on that consideration and actually leave indicated a degree of personal turmoil bordering on distraction. Individuals did leave from time to time during first year and their departures were always shrouded in secrecy. Boys who were leaving were told not to tell anybody, not to talk about their intentions with any of their peers. Consequently, when a 'leaving' took place it was like a death. One minute they were there, maybe one's best friend, and the next minute they were gone, with no goodbyes. Usually the person leaving was spirited away while the rest of us were at Mass in the morning. When we returned to the dormitory after Mass, a cubicle would be cleared out, the blankets folded and one of our former friends would have simply vanished. He was never spoken of again by those in authority and when his former colleagues spoke of him, they did so in whispers. The sense of dread which lingered about the place for days afterwards spoke eloquently of the widely held belief that something of deadly significance has just occurred.

In later years, I would look back at those days and realise that while I had been completely indoctrinated by the teaching on vocations, some of the other boys were not so impressionable, and that for them to leave the Juniorate was no more traumatic than moving to a new secondary school. Occasionally, while out on one of our Sunday walks, we would bump into one of our former colleagues. On those occasions, we were directed to pass by without speaking; communicating with 'externs' was not allowed.

SECOND YEAR IN BALDOYLE

My second year in Baldoyle was much the same as the first, apart from the fact that I was more familiar with the routine; this year there would be no surprising events waiting to ambush me. We did, however, have the satisfaction of witnessing the opening of a brand new concert hall, which was under construction during my first year. Now we would have a proper stage with lighting, curtains and flats, on which to stage our music and drama.

The steady tramp of our daily existence was marked by a continuation of prayer and study, broken now and then by a small celebration to mark a particular feast day or some other cause for rising above the humdrum. A celebration of this type was called a 'Gaudy', short for the Latin word '*Gaudeamus*', meaning 'let us rejoice'.

On a Gaudy day, dinner was accompanied by a bottle of lemonade and at tea time each boy got five Cleeve's sweets, an orange and a Crunchie. For boys whose food was good and plentiful but never extravagant, this was luxury in the extreme. The custom of the Gaudeamus Days would last for all the remaining years that we would spend in the houses of formation.

In a rather futile attempt to improve the diction of his young charges, Br Paul engaged the services of an elocution teacher, who was also a well-known actor and theatre expert. This man held classes every week and tried to iron out the many regional quirks inherited from the varied environments from which the boys came. It became clear, very early in the exercise and as a surprise to many, that the boys from the west spoke the best English. We Midlanders flattened all the vowel sounds beyond recognition, while the Northerners turned each vowel sound into two distinct sounds. The Dubliners, of course, had their 'dis' and their 'dat'. The whole exercise, however, will be remembered for the degree of hilarity it engendered, with the whole group collapsing in merriment at each valiant attempt to speak the Queen's English in a way the Queen might approve of. Eventually, the effort was abandoned and the poor elocution teacher took his undoubted skills elsewhere.

I had long been aware that, in spite of the fact that our daily sphere of existence was separated from the outside world, the group dynamic at work in our little isolated cosmos was not all that different from that which operated outside. It was a little surprising to me, therefore, to come to the realisation that, in spite of our God-centred ethos, a whole range of hierarchies established themselves in the group, decided on by factors which were not in the slightest degree God-centred or spiritual. Prowess on the hurling or football field guaranteed a high degree of status and respect, as did knowledge of the newly-born rock and pop culture of the early 1960s. So too, but to a much lesser extent, did intellectual prowess in the classroom. Physical maturity and good looks were guaranteed to rate one higher in the pecking order. Some individuals attempted to consolidate their status by forming little exclusive groups – cliques, as they were disparagingly called. Some boys exuded a tough, macho maleness, while, at the other extreme, some presented themselves as delicate, refined, sentimental and hardly male at all. This outward presentation of self had its own bearing on one's position on the social ladder, with the macho near the top and the 'butterfly' near, or at, the bottom.

A form of behaviour known as 'eye-serving' was classified as most unacceptable in Baldoyle. This occurred when a boy only behaved well while he was under the eye of someone in authority. Eye-serving was strongly disapproved of by both teachers and boys, as it implied a degree of sneakiness, cowardice and unreliability. The Brothers also listed as a major transgression the habit of 'stirring it up' – spreading discontent among one's peers. They always advised that if a cause for discontent existed, we should speak our minds to the Superior, man to man.

Second year would culminate in the Intermediate Certificate examination, and again the Brothers' approach to clear organisation and planning would come to the fore, with the house bell being rung at specific intervals during the exams to tell us when it was time to move on to the next question.

Exams put aside, it was time for us to pack our suitcases and prepare for the first of several moves through a series of houses of formation. This move would bring us to St Joseph's, Marino, on Griffith Avenue, where we would start our first year of Novitiate. So, with a lot of sadness and a little relief, we bade farewell to Baldoyle and to the men who taught us there. Given that this house had become our surrogate home and that the Brothers there were in ways our surrogate parents, leaving it behind was tantamount to leaving home all over again. And even though much of the pattern of events and practices established here would continue in all the houses we would later inhabit, in the eyes of many of the boys, myself included, there would be nowhere quite like Baldoyle and we would look back on our time spent there with great fondness. But leave it we must, and we would have to get used to moving on, for we would change houses every year for the next four years.

THE NOVITIATE

The move to the Novitiate was regarded as a highly important stage in the formation of the trainee Brothers. Here, we would experience a year of total immersion in religion, to the almost complete exclusion of all things temporal. Our contacts with home and family would continue to be kept to the absolute minimum. All letters would be monitored, as in Baldoyle. There would be no radio, television, newspapers, or books of a non-religious subject matter. Even if we had been allowed to use one, which we weren't, many of us didn't even know how to operate a telephone. The novices, as we were now called, would have no contact with the outside world. From my perspective, during the twelve months between the summer of 1961 and the summer of 1962, the outside world ceased to exist and I had neither knowledge of, nor interest in, anything that happened during that time. That the world flirted dangerously with nuclear war over Cuba, that Adolf Eichmann was hanged and Nelson Mandela jailed, that Telstar was launched – none of this was noticed by our little group, as we directed all our attention on our religious training.

Our year would start with two events of great symbolic significance: we would receive the habit, or uniform, of the Christian Brothers and we would discard our own Christian names and adopt a 'name in religion', which we would use from that moment on, along with the prefix Br or Bro. The discarding of our old clothes and old names brought home, in a powerful way, the fact that we were entering a situation and a state of mind of otherworldliness, as well as moving several steps closer to full membership of the Christian Brothers' organisation. This was to be a new existence which was God-centred and spirit-centred, and the things of the outside world were no longer of any great importance.

Thirty-one boys entered the Novitiate with me in the summer of 1961. I was now fifteen years of age. We immediately set about the business of preparing for our 'Reception', that is, the ceremony of receiving the habit and adopting our new name. Each novice was allowed to pick three names – names of saints – and from this list the Novice Master picked one. The name I ended up with happened to be my third choice, Br Paulinus. In addition, we were measured for our habits. We would be supplied with a new one, for formal wear, and also a second-hand one for day-to-day use. We wondered, as we tried out various used habits for size, what became of their former owners. We were soon to find out. Of the thirty-two boys who started the year in Marino, one in four would leave by the time the year ended – hence the ownerless, second-hand habits.

The habit consisted of an ankle-length tunic, which buttoned down the front and was held around the waist by a wide belt or cincture. A black stock surmounted by a white half-collar circled the neck and hung down over the upper chest. Each novice was given a small crucifix, called the Mission Cross, which was suspended around the neck inside the habit. We were given large black rosary beads, which would become our *vade mecum* for as long as we remained in the Order, and a voluminous cloak which we wore over the habit during inclement weather.

The ceremony itself was very moving; an apt beginning to a year that was, all in all, a deeply spiritual experience. Whether it prepared the novices for the life ahead of them, or any life for that matter, was unclear. The choral work for the ceremony was performed by the novices who had just finished their first year of Novitiate and were now starting on their second year. No 'externs' or family members were invited.

At this time, the supply of would-be trainee Christian Brothers was very plentiful, with between thirty and forty boys entering Novitiate each year in the northern half of the country, while an equal, if not bigger number entered in the southern half. The fact that so many dropped out along the way wasn't so significant, therefore, from the Brothers' perspective, given the plentiful supply.

The regime in the Novitiate was akin to the everyday lives of contemplative monks. The novices arose early, five forty-five, and went down to the chapel for morning prayers, meditation and Mass. Part of the meditation time was spent outdoors, when we could be seen walking about in the early morning darkness, wrapped in our cloaks. Breakfast followed, in silence, while one of the group read aloud from a spiritual book. After breakfast, the housekeeping was attended to, with each novice looking after his own assigned charge. Much of the day was spent in spiritual reading and study, and attending talks on spirituality and the religious life, given by the Novice Master. An hour was set aside in the afternoon for games – football or handball. This was the first time in the day that we were allowed to speak to one another. In this house, the boys were expected to take part in 'manual work', which could be anything from gardening, farming, building, painting and decorating, or even raking up leaves only to watch the wind blow them away again. As in Baldoyle and all the other houses of formation in which I would spend time, each boy was expected to take his turn working in the kitchen, helping the Brother who did all the cooking. We did two days at a time, being allowed to absent ourselves from whatever activities were being engaged in by the rest of the group. In this way, we all absorbed some knowledge of basic cooking skills, which would at least keep us from starving in later life.

Silence permeated the twenty-four hours of the day, with speaking being allowed only during games, walks and during a short period of 'recreation' at night-time. Each boy had a face-to-face conference with the Novice Master on a regular basis during the year, at which personal guidance was given, as well as advice and correction where such was deemed necessary. The option to attend piano and violin classes continued here and I belatedly opted to learn the violin.

Apart from these peripheral aspects to life in the Novitiate, the main focus was on the Religious Life and the personal spiritual development it required. This dealt with the boys' understanding of life as a Religious, with their practice of that life, and with preparation for the Religious Life stretching out ahead of them, as working, serving Christian Brothers. The model or template of a Christian Brother was clearly laid down and established in the Constitution or Book of Rules by which they lived their lives and also by an astonishing internal document called 'The Directory of the Christian Brothers'. This latter laid down precise directives concerning every minute detail of the life and living of a Christian Brother: the type of person a Christian Brother should be; how he should behave himself in every aspect of his life, and how he should cope with the world outside the Order and with those with whom he might come into contact.

Again, as in Baldoyle, the emphasis here was on making each individual fit the template, which was so clearly delineated. If there was an acceptance of allowing, encouraging or facilitating the personal growth of each individual according to their own personal template, then it wasn't immediately obvious. Other Religious Orders did not have a defined role or function, going wherever they saw a need or an opening for their particular talents, all in the context of serving their fellow men and their God. But in the Brothers' Order, the role was defined and specified. They were to serve man and God as teachers.

Significantly, one of the five vows by which they would live their lives related to the 'gratuitous instruction of the poor'. So it was the role of all the houses of formation to produce young men who would fit this template. To a degree, this could be seen as 'mass production of Religious', where one template fitted all or, more properly, all must fit the one template. Those who didn't or wouldn't fit this template were regarded as the failures and could be discarded or simply be allowed to drop away.

The amount of coercion that was required to carry out this metamorphosis depended on the person involved. In some cases, it demanded a lot of effort and pressure, in an ongoing battle to replace the old and worldly with the new and unworldly. In other cases, as in mine, so convinced was I of the truth and worth of the training I had received up to this, and was still receiving, that it was I who applied the pressure to turn myself into the perfect Christian Brother. By now, I had no difficulty coping with the silence, the isolation from family and the outside world, the huge emphasis on prayer, meditation, correction and study. I relished the almost spartan lifestyle, the lack of luxuries and its aspiration towards high, spiritual ideals. The stark honesty of the regime attracted me, where what was professed was practised and what was said was meant. Other boys found this existence impossible to bear, so there was a steady stream of departures. By the time the summer of 1962 came around, the number in the group had dropped to twenty-four. The austere life as followed in the Novitiate may have led some of the boys to believe that this was what life would be like as a serving Christian Brother but as I was to learn in later years, this was far from being the case. I would eventually discover that the life of a serving Christian Brother was in no way similar to the lifestyle as followed by the novices and that, ironically, their leaving may have been ill-advised, if not unnecessary.

The Novice Master was a saintly man called Br Luke, who did his best to mould the boys as was expected of him by his Order. He passed on a profound appreciation and respect for the spiritual life. His dealings with the novices were kind and fatherly but at all times firm. Where he encountered behaviour or attitudes which he regarded as unacceptable, he was uncompromising in his correction. His favourite saying was, 'Don't kick if I kick! If you're worth keeping you're worth correcting. I don't waste time picking spots out of rotten apples!'

The training in the Novitiate was very intense and highly personal. The year was interspersed with retreats – days dedicated totally to religious matters, talks, prayers, confession, meditation and reading, all conducted in absolute silence and presided over by an outside facilitator. Some of the retreats were for one day, while others were for three days, and the year culminated in an eight-day retreat. At the heart of much of the teaching the novices received was the never-ending struggle against the world, the flesh and the Devil. To this end, the novices took part in an exercise called 'Accusation of Faults', in which each would be required to kneel in front of the Novice Master in the presence of his peers and accuse himself of whatever faults or sins he had committed. He then had to remain on his knees to receive a lecture on the sins in question.

There was a distrust of the emotional and a boosting of the intellectual. Religious experiences that arose as an emotional response were regarded as being less worthy than those from an intellectual source. Far from being in touch with our emotions and being easy with their expression, we were urged to bring our emotions under the control of our minds.

As part of this ongoing battle against one's humanity, the use of 'the Discipline' was introduced, but only on a voluntary basis. The Discipline was, in fact, a small whip consisting of several knotted leather thongs with which a person was intended to beat himself across the naked back as a form of self-punishment, in order to do penance for his sinfulness and to bring under control his 'lower' nature. The swish and smack of these things could be heard routinely in the dormitory at night. Being at least as idealistic as everyone else, I asked for and was given the Discipline. I used it only once and, finding it such a horrendous experience, I decided that the only future use for my whip would be to lace up my boots. One of my colleagues, however, had established quite a reputation for the energetic use of his Discipline, only to have the myth exploded when someone peeped through his curtains to observe him knocking seven bells out of his pillow! How the pillow had sinned to deserve such punishment was anyone's guess!

Some of the novices did carry this policy of self-denial to unwise and dangerous levels. Among a small group, quite extreme forms of fasting became prevalent. It was common to observe individuals endlessly toying with their food, cutting it up and moving it around their plate, but never appearing to eat it. Weight loss was marked in some cases and the Novice Master had to speak to some people to get them to resume sensible eating patterns.

TAKING VOWS

As the Novitiate year moved on, the emphasis of the teaching shifted to preparation for taking the vows of the Christian Brothers' Order. The occasion of taking the vows would officially mark the entry of the young men to full membership of the Order. The Brothers took five vows, the usual three of Poverty, Chastity and Obedience, which most other Religious Orders also took, and an additional two, Perseverance in the Congregation and the Gratuitous Instruction of the Poor. Vows were taken initially for one year, at the end of which there was a short period of reflection on the part of the individual and also on the part of the Order. Everything being to the satisfaction of both parties, the vows were taken again for the next year. This meant that if a person wished to leave the Order there was an opportunity to do so. To leave at any other time during the year would require a dispensation from the Vatican. On reaching their twenty-fifth year, the Brothers were invited to take final vows, which were taken for life. A dispensation from Rome would be necessary if anyone decided to leave after taking final vows.

Religious vows were solemn and binding promises made to God to live one's life according to defined principles. The vow of Poverty was a promise to live life in a way detached from worldly goods. The vow of Chastity promised a life of celibacy and purity. Obedience implied obedience to the Order's Constitution and also to one's Superiors. In an additional, unnecessary gesture, given the huge emphasis on following one's vocation and the very specific edicts in the Constitution relating to leaving the Order, the Brothers also took a vow to Persevere in the Congregation. The final vow also had outlived its meaning to an extent. They promised Gratuitous Instruction of the Poor at a time when the State paid for all education (at least at primary level and would soon be doing so at second level).

And so, the emphasis in the latter part of the first year of Novitiate focused on the vows, their meaning, how they would influence the lives of the people who would take them, and also on the significance of finally becoming members of the Brothers' Order. The ceremony of taking of the vows, or 'Profession', as it was called, was a hugely solemn and meaningful one. Again, my colleagues and I were not allowed to invite any friends or family members but by now I had become so disassociated from home and family that this didn't present itself as any great imposition.

Looking back over the three years that I had then spent with the Brothers, one element of personal training which was noticeable by its complete absence was the area of sex education. It would appear that since the understanding was that each and every one of us would eventually take a vow of Chastity, which would imply us turning our back on marriage and sex, it was no longer a matter that needed to be addressed in any way. As far as the Christian Brothers were concerned, sex was simply 'not for us', so consequently it was not afforded any formal time or attention, apart from a veiled invitation that if anybody had 'any little questions' they might raise them during the private conference with the Novice Master. Other than that, we were left to formulate our own attitudes in this area and cope with it as best we could.

MOUNT
ST MARY, BRAY

First vows successfully in place, the newly professed Brothers – for Brothers we now were – packed up their suitcases again and said goodbye to the kind men who had looked after their welfare for the past year. This time, the move was southwards to a house outside the town of Bray in County Wicklow. This was a new, purpose-built house called Mount St Mary, in which we would continue our formation during the second year of Novitiate. This year would be slightly less intense than first year and would involve a small amount of not-too-strenuous study for our upcoming Leaving Certificate exam. The main focus of the year, however, would be a continuation of the religious training.

Our group was joined by one of a similar size from the southern province. These young men would have just professed their first vows too, having finished their first year of Novitiate in St Helen's, Booterstown. The range of accents was about to broaden dramatically, as my friends and I got to know Brothers from Cork, Kerry, Limerick, Waterford, Clare, Tipperary and from the southern counties of Leinster.

The merging of two groups who were at the same stage in their formation should have been a very easy process, but to my amazement it proved to be quite difficult. Each group had been trained in different situations by different people, who employed differing methods with differing emphases, with the result that there was a sizeable variation in attitude as well as practice in the day-to-day living out of our religious lives. As a consequence, an uneasy struggle ensued between the two groups for a couple of months. This surprised me greatly, since I was, from my first days in Baldoyle, inclined to accept as absolute all the teaching I had been given. In my youthful and inexperienced mind, what I had been taught was the truth and this truth was unquestionable. Here, I was meeting people who had a different way and different opinions. However, we soon learned to live with each other's differences. This could possibly be seen as an unanticipated learning experience for boys who had been educated in an extremely narrow and restrictive manner.

An unexpected corollary for me, of this small internal struggle between differing viewpoints, was the realisation and acceptance that there could be another way and that perhaps the absolutism of our teaching to date need not necessarily be beyond question. For this reason, the year of second Novitiate was not a particularly happy one, since absolutes are always much easier to deal with than uncertainties. I was now in my sixteenth year and was beginning to allow myself to question what I was being told. I was also maturing physically and the blasé acceptance of celibacy was beginning to take on possible consequences that I hadn't dreamed of earlier on. A preoccupation with sin and the propensity towards evil in humankind provided an uncomfortable and unforgiving environment for a young man to grow in self-knowledge and self-understanding. At times, during this year, I fleetingly questioned myself as to the direction in which I was being lead, but the ever-present and oft-repeated admonition about the dangers of losing one's vocation didn't allow me to pursue these questionings for very long.

Mount St Mary was a new house, with none of the ancient cosiness of the other two places in which I had lived since leaving home. I missed the sense of inherited permanence that we had experienced in the older houses. Surprisingly, I also missed the uncompromising asceticism of my first year in Novitiate, with all its philosophical thought and directed study. In a way, I regarded everything in this new house as being a diluted version, which I found somewhat unsatisfying. It was almost as if I had arrived at a level of religious stoicism in Marino but here I was being told that that level was not necessary. It was now enough to obey the Rule and say one's prayers. Whatever doubts I had, however, I was content to remain silent and just get on with life as it presented itself. I was, as yet, unwilling to even consider the momentous thought that perhaps there was another way to live my life. Consequently, when the summer of 1963 approached and it was time to apply to my Superiors for permission to take my vows for the second time, I had little hesitation in so doing. In due course, then, in the cavernous chapel of Mount St Mary, my colleagues and I committed ourselves by vows to live the life of Christian Brothers for another year.

COLÁISTE CHIARÁIN, BRAY

Our next move was across the fields to a neighbouring house called Coláiste Chiaráin. The sole focus in this place was to prepare for the Leaving Certificate examination. If there existed a building diametrically different from Mount St Mary this was it. The house consisted of three sections. The part containing the entrance hall, reception room, chapel, some upstairs bedrooms for the staff, and a refectory downstairs in the basement, was the original house. It was very old and quite run down but it still had some antique elegance about it. The chapel had originally been the ballroom. Attached to this was a vast barn of a building with all the architectural grandeur of a cattle wintering shed. This was the study and also the recreation hall. Joined to this was a similar barn of a building, which housed the young Brothers' dormitory.

The central heating of the original building was never extended to the study or the dormitory and I frequently found it necessary to break the ice on my washbasin before I could wash and shave in the mornings. The study, however, was heated by a massive iron wood-burning stove, which devoured timber like a dragon, but heated the vast room very efficiently. In the dormitory, it was often necessary to provide an assortment of basins and potties to catch the drops of water from the leaky roof, especially when the snow, which blew into the roof vents, began to thaw. Both the winters of 1963 and '64 were harsh in the extreme, so the endurance of the young men was well tested. I liked this place, though, much more so than Mount St Mary, for all its architectural limitations.

Preparation for the Leaving Certificate was the central focus of life here and it was planned that the Brothers would sit the exam after one year of full-time study. It was confidently presumed that everyone would be successful in earning a place in the Brothers' own Teacher Training College, so the pace of study was frenetic and sustained over the course of the year. Again, the curriculum offered no choices. Everyone studied the same subjects. Like Baldoyle, the teaching was clear and simple; the students were taught what they needed to be taught. We studied Irish, English, Latin, Maths (pass level only), Geography, History, Science (Botany) and Technical Drawing. The Irish language became the *lingua franca* of the house and it was relatively rare to hear a conversation in English. This was just as well, as it was around this time that the Oral Irish Exam (An Béal Scrúdú) was introduced. Our group would have set a screamingly high standard at oral Irish for the rest of the country to aspire to.

Classwork and study took up most of the day in Coláiste Chiaráin, with everything else, even prayer, being allotted only whatever time as was strictly necessary. The amount of course content being crammed home in such a short timescale meant that the students had to study almost all the time. Some opted out of games, some studied after lights out, with the help of a torch, some even resorted to secreting books on their laps while they ate their meals. Some of the young men found the regime very demanding as they applied their somewhat limited learning ability to the enormous task at hand.

All subjects were studied through the medium of Irish, with the exception of English and Latin. Rote learning again became a central pillar of the work, with one teacher in particular insisting that *everything* should be committed to memory – chunks of prose and poetry, and even vast swathes of Shakespearean commentary, to say nothing of entire mathematical questions and solutions. This method caused endless problems because some students simply could not memorise pages and pages of content and others were manly enough or sensible enough to refuse to do so. And so, the sight of individuals standing outside the classroom door, having been refused entry because they had failed to recite some solution on Stoic Agus Scaracha (Stocks & Shares) or some extract from *Bradley's Arnold*, was common enough.

That this idiocy was allowed to continue by the Superior amazed me, just as I was bewildered by the same type of inaction in Baldoyle. However, in spite of this aggravation, life was good in Coláiste Chiaráin and the students went about their momentous task with almost heroic zeal. Their single-mindedness and uncluttered focus was matched by that of their teachers, and both parties viewed the limitations in both time and facilities as a challenge. To rise above the difficulties and to aim for lofty goals became the driving force and ethos of the house. I was to learn from this experience that sometimes the most arid of gardens can produce the most spectacular of blooms, and that creativity will often be found where circumstances are most unpromising.

THE LEAVING CERTIFICATE EXAMINATION

As exam time approached, we pooled our resources and worked in groups, with the stronger students sometimes adopting weaker ones and helping them along the way. The date for the Béal Scrúdú arrived and the students were ushered in, one by one, with great trepidation. Considering that their standard and ease in oral Irish was so advanced that they were now dreaming in Irish, the exam would be no problem.

As the written exam's date loomed ever nearer, ominous signs of conflict between the secondary teachers' union and the Department of Education became evident. The secondary teachers were to supervise and correct the Leaving Certificate examination; for them to go on strike at this time would have serious consequences for the students. Negotiations eventually did break down and the union withdrew the services of its members, banning all supervision and correction work. From the point of view of the students in Coláiste Chiaráin, the impasse was resolved satisfactorily when the INTO, the primary teachers' union, issued a directive to its members allowing them to step into the breach – effectively strike breaking. So the exam of 1964 went ahead, supervised and corrected by primary teachers and practically anyone else who could satisfy the Department of Education that they had the ability to do so – whether they had or not.

The supervisor in our school was an extremely nervous primary teacher who patrolled up and down between the rows of desks as if expecting to find texts and notes hidden about the person of each student. Several boys from a local second-level school in Bray also sat their exam in Coláiste Chiaráin. One of these caused amazement and some merriment by arriving each day with copious notes, facts, dates, figures and formulae scribbled on both forearms and both legs. These he openly referred to in moments of difficulty by pulling up his shirt sleeves or his trouser leg. The supervisor, for all his suspicions, failed to spot any of this.

The exam ran its course and we had time to give some thought to the question of our annual vows. For me, the intensity and industry of the year had blotted from my consciousness any of the unease which had occasionally disturbed my equilibrium during the previous year. There was no moment of doubt in my mind now. I would ask permission to take my third vows, committing myself to another year as a Christian Brother.

And while our year in this particular little microcosm came to an end, another world away the Second Vatican Council was drawing to a close and would soon be announcing changes in the understanding and practices of the Church, which would, if and when they were introduced, have a significant effect on the future of the Church and its members. These changes would have very little effect on the lives of the Brothers about to leave Coláiste Chiaráin, for the immediate future at least, and they might be forgiven for believing that their world would never change. However, it would only be a few years before the Brothers would gather in Special General Chapter to rewrite their entire Constitution, taking on board the new thinking of the Council.

With our vows taken and our Leaving Certificate finished, we packed our possessions again for the final move of our training, this time back to Marino, but to a different building – St Mary's Christian Brothers' Teacher Training College.

TEACHER
TRAINING
IN MARINO

Almost immediately, a number of events occurred which would have a profound effect on me. Firstly, the Director of the Training College who had looked after the young Brothers' cohort in previous years, having finished his stint in that role, moved on to 'fresh fields' and his place was taken by an elderly Brother who apparently had no experience of dealing with trainee Brothers who also happened to be young men. I was eighteen years old by now; I was used to being treated as an adult and expected no less. I had, after all, been making life decisions for myself since I was thirteen. The new Superior failed to realise this and set about instituting a regime of freedom limitation that would have seen me and my colleagues revert to a situation much like that which was in vogue in our early days in Baldoyle. As a response to this, the young trainees embarked on a campaign of disobedience and non-co-operation, which resulted in a very unsettled and unhappy atmosphere in the house.

At the height of this development, I and two of my colleagues were summoned to the Director's office to be told that since we had achieved good results in our Leaving Certs, we were being sent to University College, Dublin, to study for a degree, with the intention that we would eventually go to the North of Ireland to teach at secondary level there. Brothers in those days were expected to take their orders from their Superiors without demur and so, accordingly, we three were equipped with a bicycle each, a bag and directions to Earlsfort Terrace, to begin our university education.

UCD – ON A BIKE

Our initial sortie across the city on our bikes had all the
breathtaking gravitas of Shackleton's expedition to the
South Pole; three young men who had rarely seen the
outside of an enclosed monastery for the past five years,
in their long black coats and their black hats, atop three
ancient bicycles, pedalling assiduously in the middle of
the city traffic and stopping now and then to consult
their map. We coped as best we could with the vagaries
of the traffic and the city, only to be confronted by the
magic and the mysteries of university life. Here there
were choices to be made, faculty choices and subject
choices, where in our previous lives there had been no
choices. As had been our practice to date, all three of us
chose the same faculty – Arts, and the same subjects –

English and Latin at honours level, and Maths and Irish at pass level.

And so, with some trepidation, we embarked on our new experience, glad to escape the unhappy atmosphere of the Training College, and excited and terrified by the novelty of all that lay ahead of us. Back in Marino, we were each assigned a small room, as opposed to the curtained cubicles which the other Brothers still occupied. We were now a little group apart, following our own agenda. Each morning we set off on our trek across the city to arrive in Earlsfort Terrace for the day's lectures. This was the centre of most of UCD's activities at the time, since their new campus at Belfield hadn't yet opened. Soon we developed our own individual timetables for the day, as we began to avail ourselves of the library and study facilities.

To me, it was as if I had spent the previous five years in a darkened building and all of a sudden, the doors and windows were flung open to allow the light and life to flood in. I absolutely loved the experience; the university itself but also the process of getting there and returning home again. This was the autumn of 1964 and Dublin was beginning to swing with new vibrancy and vigour. Oblivious to the image I portrayed as I pedalled along, I wallowed in the flow and flux of the throbbing city. I gazed with starved eyes at the beauty of the buildings and the beauty of the people, and revelled in it all. The old dictat of 'custody of the eyes' was jettisoned with enthusiasm as I drank in all the new experiences of sight and sound that surrounded me. The sun appeared to be always shining. In later years, I would look back on my first year of university and of the outside world and remark that I had no memory of it ever raining.

In college, I marvelled at the wide-open range of the courses and the manner in which the lecturers broadened the scope of the specific topics to establish connections between literature, history and society, between Irish, English and European literature, between mathematics and life, between Latin and modern languages. It was as if, for the first time, knowledge in its broadest possible meaning was being presented as a vast unlimited whole, whereas before it was divided and subdivided into many separate compartments. I spent hours in the college library reading avidly, as one topic lead me on to the next and from there to the next. I visited many of the Dublin city libraries and savoured their differences and their specialisms. In locating the libraries, I became familiar with the topography and shape of the city and I relished it all.

This exposure to a new style of educating caused me to review the previous five years of my own education.

I had no difficulty recognising the strengths. These were many and obvious. The classroom teaching was spare and to the point, designed in such a way as to make learning as efficient and manageable as possible, and also to facilitate the passing of examinations effectively. What the instruction possessed in efficiency however, it lacked in width and depth, with the content honed and chiselled to the absolute, essential elements. That said, though, what I had learned, I had learned well and much of it would stay with me, something I would appreciate greatly in later life. Other elements of my learning experience were much less formal and more incidental, growing out of the many extra-curricular experiences I was gifted with during my school days. These included a nurtured interest in and aptitude for music, as well as a broad range of musical appreciation; a taste for hands-on making and doing, fed from the well-spring of the varied forms of manual work in which we engaged; the invaluable education gleaned from the social interaction with boys from many different backgrounds and homes, and the thinking skills fed by years of lectures, readings, meditations and introspection, which equipped me with a degree of stoicism and durability that would stand to me during the rest of my life.

On the other hand, I was aware of the lack of social interaction with normal society, especially heterosexual companionship. I was also conscious of my emotional immaturity, which I saw as stemming from the Brothers' somewhat tough and 'no-nonsense' attitude to this aspect of human life. Emotions were meant to be controlled or suppressed and were not allowed to get in the way of the practical work to be done. At the time of my passing through the system, a cry for help would more likely be responded to with, 'Pull yourself together and snap out of it', rather than, 'Sit down and tell me about it.' I also noticed in myself a lack of tolerance towards my fellow man, or woman as the case might be, which I felt arose from a sense of distrust in my own humanity and subsequently in other people. This was something I would struggle with in later life.

During my first year in university, I read and studied so widely and so much, that when the summer exams came around, I found I lacked sufficient focus to answer adequately the questions set by the lecturers. I found that I knew so much – but not the specific answers to the specific questions. When the results came out I found that I had passed everything but had failed to get honours in either English or Latin.

CHANGING DIRECTION

The results, however, didn't really concern me much, because, to my amazement, I had undergone a major change of mind regarding my future. Imperceptibly, over the course of the year, I had begun to allow myself to consider the possibility that maybe my future didn't lie in the Christian Brothers. So preoccupied was I with all my new experiences, that the gradual change had happened almost unknown to me. During the year, I had given scant consideration to the question of my vocation, but as the time approached for making a decision about taking vows again for a fourth year, I found that a decision had almost made itself. I now felt, without a shadow of doubt, that I needed to leave the Christian Brothers and to join the real world I had so recently sampled. As the days advanced ever nearer to decision time, I agonised and worried about my dilemma. The teaching I had absorbed so dutifully over the previous six years, from various teachers and preachers, about the terrible eternal consequences of 'losing one's vocation' was as vivid and as traumatic as it ever was. To ignore it now, I feared, or to act in direct contravention of it, would have consequences so serious that I would spend the rest of my life, and indeed eternity, in suffering. In spite of this awareness, however, my attitude towards my own involvement in religious life had changed – when and how, I wasn't sure, but imperceptibly, change had occurred.

When the time came for applying for the next year of annual vows, I had more or less decided that I was going to leave and to take my chances with the fires of hell. I wasn't sure if my decision was to leave the Christian Brothers' Order or to join the newly discovered 'real world'. It was possibly a combination of both. One thing I did know, however, was the fact that as long as I was 'behind the walls', isolated from the outside world and cocooned in the little insular existence of the houses of formation, it was as if there was a curtain between me and certain realities, and it was only when I mixed with real people in the outside world that these realities became clear. What's more, in lots of ways I felt that I had moved away from the ideals and practices of First Novitiate and the life as we were now living it just didn't suit me any more. I wasn't at all sure how I had come to this way of thinking or feeling, but I now felt that this life wasn't for me. I had moved past the realm of what I 'wished to do' into the realm of what I 'needed to do' over the course of a very short time. So now I was faced with the enormity of leaving Religious Life.

From the vantage point of today, leaving Religious Life probably appears quite a simple thing to do, but back in 1965 it was an enormous decision to make. On the one hand, I would have to deal with the religious implications of losing my vocation, and on the other, I would have to live with the public perception of a defector from a Religious Order. In the outside world, there was the unspoken disapproval of laicisation, the 'spoiled priest' or the failed Religious. I would have to run the gauntlet of public disapproval, which I knew would be waiting for me. Be that as it may, however, by the end of my first year in university I had decided that I was going to leave the Order.

I had no idea what life 'outside' would be like. I had missed out on everything that would normally happen between the ages of thirteen and twenty. I was afraid that I wouldn't be able to fit in in normal society. Would I be able to earn a living? I had no qualifications yet, just First Arts. My parents couldn't afford to support me in college so I would have to get a job. I also had to succeed in getting into college for night lectures. I didn't know anything about any of this. Furthermore, I wondered about my ability to form relationships, especially romantic relationships. Would I be able to father a family? After all those years of repression I wasn't sure if all my 'bits' would work as nature intended! My knowledge of the fairer sex had been more or less confined to the Blessed Virgin. I had never spoken to a girl, much less had a relationship with one. And while the whole prospect filled me with terror, I still knew that leave I must.

My first job was to tell my parents, which I absolutely dreaded. That they would be disappointed in their 'spoiled Religious' of a son, I was sure. I had it all rehearsed, the exact words I was going to use at their next visit, but unfortunately, when the time came, the mask slipped and I bawled and blubbered my way through my terrible confession. My parents were very understanding about it and that made me cry all the more. My mother certainly was delighted with the news, I was to learn later. Dad was quite pleased too, although he didn't show it.

TEACHING

Before my plans had the opportunity to advance, an unexpected development catapulted me out of the house of formation that had been my home for the past year. A young Brother who had completed his first year of teaching had decided to leave suddenly, and since the school year didn't finish until the middle of July, I was sent to take his place for the remaining five or six weeks of the term. Unencumbered by either training or experience, I found myself confronting fifty nine-year-old boys in class 3B in St Paul's CBS, North Brunswick Street, in the centre of Dublin City. My job was to teach them their Irish, English, Arithmetic, Religious Knowledge and Singing – as best as I knew how.

To be moved so precipitously from the world of academia to this hive of activity was quite a shock, but a pleasant experience nonetheless. I thought that the boys were marvellous, with a naivety and innocence that really surprised me. They had no shyness about them and had an awful lot to say. It delighted me to listen to them babble away about everything in their experience, without the slightest wariness or distrust in their listener. Because I had neither training nor experience, the school principal felt the need to show the way, to demonstrate the accepted methodology for teaching in this school at this time. He also observed and guided me in my first faltering steps in the business of teaching. I valued his advice and direction – and indeed his correction, where deemed necessary – and I had a good working relationship with the gruff Kerryman.

This was indeed a long way from Killough National School in County Westmeath, which was my last direct contact with primary education. The standards and ambitions in 'Brunner', as it was called, were high and demanding, and this called for an equally high rate of preparation and delivery from the teachers. What did shock me was the frequency and the severity of the corporal punishment in the form of the strap. I soon realised that in an environment where these levels were significant, even the students came to expect it, so that the option to be an 'easy' or a 'soft' teacher didn't really exist.

So I felt that I needed to use it too if I wanted to be taken seriously, and it was, in later life, a source of real regret and sorrow to me to admit to myself that I had used the strap too often and too vigorously. Many a time I would look back on those days and hope that the children I dealt with would forgive me for my severity and see my self-perceived excesses as the norm for the time.

Having told my Provincial Superior by letter that I wanted to leave when my current vows expired in the summer, I was summoned to his office. The Brother Provincial was a nice man named Brother Mulholland who listened sympathetically to my story. He suggested that I might give it one more year, 'Go out and live the life of a Brother, teach in a school and then make a decision.' This course of action was, in fact, the normal one followed by young Brothers, who would be sent out to teach as untrained assistants for a number of years before being summoned back to Marino to complete year two of their training. It is obvious that a few years of hands-on experience 'at the chalkface', so to speak, would be valuable for trainee teachers as they approached the second half of their training.

Now that I had told all the people I needed to tell and that my awful secret was shared with a few people, I felt that the pressure was off me a bit and I was quite pleased to take Br Mulholland's advice. I thought that it would give me more time and space to make up my mind, to plan my course and to prepare the ground. My willingness to long-finger the decision to leave may have also indicated that I wasn't, in fact, ready to go just yet. One didn't fly against the face of heaven without having all the angles thought out. I needed to come to some sort of reconciliation with my tortured conscience and form some rationale that would enable me to face the rest of my life, and indeed eternity, with some degree of equanimity. And then there always was the possibility that life 'on the mission', as the working life of the Brothers was called, might impress me so strongly that I would change my mind and recover my lost vocation. Consequently, I saw the year ahead as a critical milestone in my life plan. The decisions I would make during this year would plot the life stretching out ahead of me, and I was glad to have additional time and space in which to make them.

A HOLIDAY IN
THE REAL WORLD

When the school year in Brunner finally ended in mid-July 1965, I was allowed home for a short visit, the first such holiday in five years. When I was last at home I was fourteen years of age, now I was nineteen. Because I had been contemplating a return to the 'outside world', I found, to my amazement, that I no longer felt as out of place as I had done when previously at home. Now I was observing and trying to be part of a world I had regarded as being alien and not for me when last I viewed it. I felt a degree of welcome and warmth in the society of ordinary people. So relaxed did I become that I even accepted and smoked my first cigarette!

What amazed me most, however, was the smallness of the house, the rooms and the garden. I had become accustomed to massive buildings with long corridors, spacious halls and sweeping stairways that accessed many storeys. My old home consisted of four normal-sized rooms – normal by usual standards but not by the standards of the institutions I had called home for the past six years. I found it a bit claustrophobic and was thankful for the great outdoors, which afforded me some personal space.

My mind was in a state of total confusion. I was on the cusp of deciding whether I was a Religious Brother or a secular layman. Almost as if testing the water, I occasionally allowed myself to be one and then the other. Knowing that I had a decision to make and that I had been afforded some additional time to do that, I tried to think and feel like a layman, as well as thinking and feeling like a Religious. While at home, I listened to the talk of family members in an attempt to enter into their world, to understand and appreciate everything that occupied their minds. Occasionally, I would borrow some clothes from one of my brothers and leave aside my black clothes in order to see how it felt to be a layman and to test other people's reaction to me as a layman. All in all, this trial run at laicisation was a successful and very worthwhile exercise, which would ease, to an extent, the decision-making that faced me.

In due course, it was time to return to Dublin to pursue my first year, and possibly my last, as a working Christian Brother, serving in a Brothers' school and living in a Brothers' community.

ON THE MISSION

It was to my satisfaction that I learned that I was being assigned again to North Brunswick Street CBS for the coming year. This was the school in which I had served earlier in the summer and had enjoyed so much. This time I was given class 2B: fifty-two eight year olds from the neighbouring streets of inner-city Dublin. I was to live in the Brothers' monastery on the North Circular Road. From there I would cycle the short journey down past Grangegorman to Brunswick Street, bag on the carrier and long black soutane flapping in the breeze. I found the boys in Brunner as I had left them a few months earlier – enthusiastic, talkative, open and unsophisticated, trusting and friendly. The class work I found testing, more because of my own lack of training and experience than anything else. Much of the time I found out the best way to do things by accidentally choosing the worst way. So for me it was necessary to learn by doing rather than by any prior knowledge or skill I brought with me into the classroom. However, my many blunders were either unnoticed or generously forgiven by the effervescent eight-year-olds in front of me.

My classroom was ridiculously overcrowded but such was the demand for places in Brunner that the Brothers tended to accept as many as they could possibly handle. At this time they were engaged in an extensive building programme to provide additional classroom space. The school was completely blocked in on all sides, either by other buildings or by the streets, and so since they couldn't expand out, they were forced to expand up. The new block of classrooms would consist of several floors standing on concrete pillars, with the existing playground running underneath. As a result, during my year in the school, the playground was a building site, with little or no play area and the constant danger of accidents. At break time, for fear that one of my charges would be run over by a dump truck or get buried without trace in a hole, I used to line them up and they would march together to the toilets singing lustily, 'We're off to Dublin in the Green, in the Green'.

Overcrowding brought with it a litany of problems which wouldn't be allowed in later times, but here and at this time, teachers did the best they could. This was a time that predated the arrival of Remedial or Special-Needs Teachers for special-needs pupils and so it was inevitable that such children would come under severe pressure in order not to be left behind. Unfortunately, the goals were the same for all and it was an obvious struggle for some boys to even approach reaching those targets. It was also an era of corporal punishment and this is a cause of much regret for me, as I look back on those days from a more enlightened time.

Difficulties aside, though, I enjoyed my year in Brunner and I would later recall my young charges with great warmth and fondness. I worked tirelessly with them, involving them in many extra-curricular activities, training them in football and hurling in the Forty Acres in the Phoenix Park after school and on Saturdays. Many of the boys had older brothers who were members of Arbour Hill Boxing Club and as a result of their pleadings I started a boxing league in my classroom. Every Friday, after class, the desks were formed into a square and two doughty youths faced up against each other, wearing massive boxing gloves, to see who would go forward to the next round. I officiated as referee and judge, hoping all the time that there would be no injuries. Eventually, the final was staged and one boy was crowned champion. Viewed from a modern perspective, obsessed by health and safety issues and dogged by insurance concerns, this was an extremely risky venture, but one that turned out reasonably well.

I would later remember with great admiration the hugely constructive Parents' Association, who threw themselves into the business of supporting the school with limitless energy.

DECISION TIME

During all this time, I never left aside the question of my own future in the Order. In the background to every new experience were the unanswered questions – Was this the life for me? Could I see myself living like this for the rest of my life? Did I actually believe in the value of this lifestyle? I played my part wholeheartedly in community life and in work, in order to test by experience how I felt about both. I confronted the whole question of vocation, believing that in order for me to make a decision in this regard, I had to formulate some understanding of vocation that would leave me free to stay or to leave. If I adhered to the old doctrine that had been taught so effectively since my first day in Baldoyle, I would have no freedom to make a decision, since that doctrine condemned anyone who left to eternal damnation. I gradually began to accept a vision of a forgiving God who recognised an honest and at times superhuman effort, but who would also smile on an honest change of mind and direction arising out of a genuine recognition that this change was wise and good and necessary. I allowed myself to believe in the notion that a vocation could be temporary and that it could lead to a fresh beginning in another direction, for the general good of mind, body and soul.

Coming to this understanding, I realised that I might have simply been fooling myself, justifying a decision already made. But in spite of this I thought and prayed long and hard in order to make a reasoned and informed decision. By the time Christmas 1965 had passed, I had made my mind up that I would leave the Brothers' Order at the end of my current vows, during the following summer. With my decision made, I applied myself for the time remaining to me as a serving Christian Brother with as much energy and as much conviction as I could summon.

The New Year of 1966 saw me continue my work in Brunner and my membership of the Brothers' community in their monastery on the North Circular Road. This latter I found particularly difficult, in that I no longer saw the life I was living as being right for me. I willingly conceded that for many other Brothers it was the perfect way to live and I privately applauded them on finding a lifestyle that suited them so well. I envied them their peace and sense of fulfilment, and occasionally wished that I could have been as contented in Religious Life. But I couldn't, so that was that.

The fact that I had made my mind up to leave didn't afford me any peace of mind, and my sense of guilt haunted me by day and by night. The traumatic internal struggle which led to my decision had been so intense that now I dreamed about it constantly. My dreams materialised the dilemma through which I had gone, always confronting me with the worst outcomes imaginable. They always portrayed conflicts and contradictions – that I was approaching the altar to get married but was still wearing the Brother's habit and collar; that I was faced by an avenging God wishing to punish me for my act of treachery in deciding to leave; that I had left and was vainly trying to get back into the monastery, which was closed against me. Most frequently I was shown that no matter which way I turned I was always going to be an incapable misfit; either a Brother who shouldn't have remained so or a layman who should still be a Brother. These dreams were to remain with me for most of my life, very frequent at first but mercifully rarer with the passage of time. They were never to disappear completely, however.

As the first months of 1966 passed by, my sense of impending doom increased, relieved only by my preoccupation with my schoolwork and the extra-curricular activities I enjoyed so much. My sense of guilt and sinfulness made it impossible to tell anybody what I intended to do, not even my closest colleagues, and rather than be hypocritical, I gradually withdrew from the company of my fellow Brothers into a world of morbid and unhappy silence.

LEAVING

But time moves on inexorably and, as the summer of 1966 approached, I felt that it was time to tell my Superior of my plans. The announcement was received with wordless disapproval, the cold silence more difficult to deal with than a blistering tirade of condemnation. A departure date was arranged and I prepared to serve out my final days as a Christian Brother. Knowing that I would be leaving behind all that constituted my home, my family and my way of life for the past seven years, made me feel incredibly sad. I hadn't expected this. I had thought that it would be a relief to leave eventually, but that was not the case. I was inconsolable as the date for departure approached, and by the time it finally arrived, I was a broken man. Removing my habit and collar for the last time was like removing my skin. In a pathetic attempt to bring something of my former life with me, and also to preserve my links with what I now feared was an affronted God, I asked my Superior if I could keep my Mission Cross and my rosary beads. The reply was a curt refusal, 'What do you want them for? If you're going, you're going!'

I carried my ancient suitcase down to the hallway, glad not to meet any of my colleagues, and waited for the taxi that would bring me and the Superior into town. We were dropped off at Clery's clothes shop on O'Connell Street, where we were spirited into a discreet back room in the company of an elderly man. It was this man's job to kit me out for my return to the sinful outside world. The almost silent manner in which this was done suggested to me that he had performed this unpleasant duty before. As I was being measured and fitted for my new secular clothes, the distaste and disapproval from the two men present were palpable. Emerging from the shop some time later in my tweed jacket, brown pants and brown shoes, I had left behind everything, including my name, that formerly identified me as a Christian Brother.

The Superior set off at a cracking pace in the direction of the railway station, pausing only once to goad me, as I struggled with my over-packed suitcase, 'This is your first taste of the outside world!' On arriving at Westland Row station, as Pearse station was then called, he handed me three £10 notes with the instruction that I should be very careful with it, as I wasn't used to handling such large sums of money! A one-way ticket to Mullingar was purchased, and my suitcase and I were deposited on the west-bound train. Cursory farewells were exchanged and then he was gone. I abruptly jumped from the train and rushed into a shop to buy ten Consulate and a box of matches, before resuming my seat. As I lit my first cigarette, I realised that my new life had just begun. I could do no more than hope for the best.

EPILOGUE

What became of me after that day is material for another story and another book. Sufficient to say that I made a good career for myself, that I was gifted with the maturing influence of a good wife, and six healthy children. I eventually dealt with the thorny question of my Christian name, opting for Lorcán, the Irish version of my first name, Laurence. Whatever emotional scars I brought with me as a result of my seven-year journey with the Christian Brothers, I have, with some considerable difficulty, learned to live with and now regard them as being not much more onerous than those carried by many other people. I have a high respect for the Christian Brothers and their work, while recognising and abhorring the negative aspects of what has come to light in recent times. My condemnation of those Brothers who abused children in their care is tempered somewhat by the realisation that, faced with similar circumstances of emotional and sexual immaturity, isolation and loneliness, who could be absolutely confident that they themselves would be without sin? While recognising that condemnation was richly warranted in many cases, I grieve for the generality of Brothers, some formerly my peers and now mostly elderly, who have been and still are subjected to an unfair and totally one-sided assault from elements of the media, despite having spent lives of deep but unspectacular sanctity and selfless dedication to their work.

I decry the Order's system of that time, of postulating and retaining its members; a system which had outlived its time and was potentially damaging to those who were subjected to it. I also condemn the failure of those in authority to recognise this and to update their practices. These included the enrolling of very young boys, barely out of primary school; the isolation of these boys from home and family and from the outside world; the intense psychological and religious pressure on the boys not to leave, and the various devices used to discourage defections, plainly unacceptable by modern standards –

devices which one would expect to encounter in the worst of present-day cults rather than in a Religious Congregation avowed to the betterment of humanity.

Just as in my own life and in society in general, time has brought the Christian Brothers knowledge and understanding, and so the destructive aspects of my formation of the 1960s, and before that, have long since been discarded and the role of the Order has broadened and deepened to the benefit of all.

While I am aware that I emerged from the Brothers' houses of formation in reasonable emotional and psychological condition, I am conscious of the fact that many others, both those who left and those who remained, weren't so fortunate and had to face life in a damaged state, with sometimes disastrous results. And while I accept, with some gratitude, the positive outcomes of my education at the hands of the Brothers, I regarded other elements of that training as being personally damaging and these required great effort and intervention, on my part and on the part of others, to counteract in later life. My parents had made me what I was, but the Brothers' formation system attempted to turn me into something else, which would conform to their own prescriptive template. What damage this personal violence did to my emerging persona I do not know but I have learned to be constantly watchful for signs of it. What I perceive as my relative good health I attribute in no small measure to the work of my parents and my family of origin, who reared me according to their own enlightenment during my childhood, equipping me with a sound value system and the inner strength I would later need for my own protection, and who accepted and supported me as I attempted to re-enter the secular world after leaving Religious Life.

As for the individuals who looked after my welfare between the ages of thirteen and twenty, with very few exceptions, I regard them as honest, dedicated and hardworking men who devoted themselves to a task and a methodology not of their own making. And if their actions, or their inactions, as the case may be, were at times misdirected and at other times plainly stupid, I see that they worked inside a structure handed down from another era, which was not necessarily suited to the one in which it was being applied.

The strong position enjoyed by the Religious Orders of that time in terms of their collective wealth, the plentiful supply of recruits and the unquestioningly high regard in which they were held by the Church and by society, lead to an over-reaching arrogance and confidence, which had the effect of blinding their vision and stunting their creativity. I recognise this; I understand it and regret its many outcomes, including the retention and operation of outmoded and damaging structures. I recognise also that the inward-looking ethos of the Brothers' Order at that time, which regarded with suspicion the outside world of Irish society, was reflected in the Irish State of the early twentieth century, which was equally inward-looking, regarding influences and practices from outside the island of 'holy' Ireland with equal suspicion. They both shared a blinkered vision, believing that anything that wasn't Gaelic and Catholic couldn't be trusted, and needed to be resisted. Perhaps in their time, and in the circumstances of that time, this was understandable, but their failure to move with the abiding and evolving spirit of the era meant that it would be left to history and experience to deliver to both a very harsh lesson.

I have rationalised the whole question of vocation to my own satisfaction, seeing in my subsequent career, my marriage and children, and now my grandchildren, the imprint of my own efforts, something more pleasing in God's eyes and more beneficial to my immediate society than would have been the case had I remained a Religious, unfulfilled, dissatisfied and unhappy.

I also recognise in the signs of the times, the zeitgeist, that the era of the Religious Orders as I knew and experienced them may be nearing its end, at least in this county and at this time, and rather than lamenting this fact, I am inclined to see in it a new emerging groundswell emanating from the people rather than from the institutional Church. The uncharted movement that is currently emptying church pews, I see as part of the same groundswell, and while for some this is a cause for upset and disappointment, for me it is the early sign of an evolving paradigm shift, which I view in much the same light as my own paradigm shift from Religious to layman. In a world which is constantly and endlessly changing, and in which people also have to be changing in order to deal with it, the idea of a vocation which deprived a human being of the freedom to make choices, to flex and change as he or she saw fit, is no longer acceptable to me. I now lay claim to the right to view my decision to leave Religious Life as as much a response to the whisperings of the Holy Spirit as was my initial decision to join all those years ago, in Killough National School, back in County Westmeath.

ADDENDUM

On the day that I finished correcting the proofs for this book a letter came to my attention. It was written by Br. Philip Pinto, the Congregational Leader of the Christian Brothers and it was addressed to all former Brothers. It marked the 250th Anniversary of the birth of Blessed Edmund Ignatius Rice, the founder of the Congregation. I reproduce the relevant section of his letter here, with his permission and without further comment. It speaks for itself:

Edmund Rice was born two hundred and fifty years ago and for the Christian Brothers and all those who have been influenced and inspired by the life of this man, it is time to pause and reflect on how we have been blessed. I remember the moment in 1996 when Edmund was beatified by Pope John Paul II in Rome. It was staggering to realise that this man born in a little rural town in an island on the west of Europe was able to impact the lives of people from all over the world. Truly, what one does with one's heart transforms the whole universe!

I wish to use this occasion today to thank all you men who walked with us for some time and then moved on in a different direction to do other things with your lives. I wish to recognise the wonderful gift you were to the Congregation and to numerous young people all over the world. So many of you have made the Congregation what it is and have given many of your best and most active years to the service of young people. Thank you for your goodness and generosity. Thank you too for remaining in touch with us in the various Provinces across the world, particularly through the difficult times we are experiencing.

I am also aware that for some of you the parting with our Congregation was painful – painful because you were letting go of something that had become part of you, painful too because we were not as gracious perhaps as we should have been. When we look back at how we lived our lives in the past we acknowledge that we were sometimes hard and unyielding and less than loving. I wish to express to you who walked with us my sorrow and regrets for the hurt and pain you endured.

If this two hundred and fiftieth anniversary is to mean anything it needs to be celebrated by humbly receiving and generously giving joy, love and forgiveness. Life is too short for anything less than living fully …

May God continue to bless you all,

Br Philip Pinto, Congregation Leader